Chef Dez
on Cooking

Volume 3

Order this book online at www.trafford.com
or email orders@trafford.com

Most Trafford titles are also available at major online book retailers.

Printed in the United States of America.

ISBN: 978-1-4669-6098-5 (sc)
ISBN: 978-1-4669-6099-2 (e)

Trafford rev. 10/11/2012

 www.trafford.com

North America & international
toll-free: 1 888 232 4444 (USA & Canada)
phone: 250 383 6864 ♦ fax: 812 355 4082

For my four children,
Corey, Krista, Noah, and Gianna . . .
may you always follow your dreams
and may your lives be blessed with
happiness

*T*o reduce the cost of this book to you, the consumer, **colour photos for the following recipes available for viewing/printing on my website at:**

www.chefdez.com

Apricot Pecan Pork Chops
Beef Barley Slowcooker Stew
Beef & Black Bean Enchiladas
Boneless Turkey Roast
Broiled Greek Tomatoes
Chick Pea Curry
Clam Chowder
Creole Halibut BBQ Pouches
Fire Roasted Corn & Black Bean Salsa
French Onion Soup
Greek Lamb Burgers
Greek Rubbed Chicken
Grilled Bacon Wrapped Meatballs
Grilled Philly Cheesesteak

Grilled Pork Chops with Apple Slaw
Honey Garlic Meat Balls
Lamb Pasta Sauce
Lamb Shanks in BBQ Sauce
Maple Mashed Sweet Potatoes
Mediterranean Olive Tofu Crostini
Mexican Casserole
Mexican Chipotle Papaya Pork
Pasta Fresca dÈstate
Pastitsio
Pear & Cranberry Cobbler
Pineapple Muesli Yogurt Parfaits
Pot Roast with Wild Mushroom Gravy
Prime Rib Roast
Rubbed & Grilled Tri Tip au Jus
Rubbed & Sauced Baby Back Ribs
Sausage & Fennel Pasta
Sausage Tomato & Herb Frittata
Slow-Cooker Pulled Pork
Slow-Cooker Thai Squash Soup
South-Western Creamed Corn
South-Western Steak Salad
Steak with Merlot Reduction
Strawberry Margarita Soy Dessert
Sundried Tomato Butter Sauce
Turkey Meatloaf

Acknowledgments

It's been three years since the release of my last book *Chef Dez on Cooking Volume Two* and I am extremely pleased to be able to offer you another great volume in this series. The fantastic feedback and demand we have received for the first two volumes made it an obvious choice to release a third. This is again another labour of love from me and my loving wife Katherine. Bringing a cookbook together is not an easy task with our hectic lifestyles. However, our shared passion for food and cooking with each other has made the journey very enjoyable, and one I would do over again in a heartbeat. I am certain that it must be challenging for her to live with someone with a career like mine, but her constant and consistent dedication and support has never waned, and for that I am so grateful. Thank you Sweetheart. She again has a chapter dedicated to her talent in baking—you will find that *"Chapter 13—Breakfast Ideas"* includes only recipes of hers.

My four incredible children: Corey, Krista, Noah, & Gianna, to whom this book is dedicated, have helped me to stay focused on what's important in life. Balancing self-employment with being a good father and husband is not an easy task and my children are a constant reminder that there is more to life than just working. With my face buried in a laptop on so many occasions, I need to thank you all for your patience and understanding. I look forward to many years of enjoyment watching you grow, learn, and become even more incredible than you are now. Thank you so much for everything and I hope at the very least that this book represents to you that a dream can grow and become reality if you want it to. Believe in yourself. You can become anything you want to become as long as you love yourself first and never give up.

Thank you Mom & Bob for your never-ending words of support and encouragement. You have always celebrated my successes with me and have never failed to tell me how proud you are of everything I do. This also is to be said about my wonderful in-laws Ron &

Bonnie Swanson. Thank you as well for your unwavering support and for being such a great part of my life. I know that our children could never have better grandparents than the four of you.

Rob & Charlotte Lepp and all the staff at *Lepp Farm Market* in Abbotsford have been, and continue to be, a huge part of my business and I love teaching classes at your incredible market. The time that Charlotte has taken out of her very busy life to write the foreword of this book speaks volumes about how much she believes in what I do. Although it is not said as much as it should be, I do appreciate everything you have done for me. Thank you so much.

Angie Quaale at *Well Seasoned Gourmet Food Store* in Langley deserves special recognition as well for her support in what I do over the past seven years. For not only welcoming me to teach on many regular occasions in her in fantastic store with her great staff, but also for having me as the official MC of the annual BBQ on the By-Pass every September. Thank you Angie.

Other people/venues where I work with and teach deserve recognition as well, such as Septembre & Raheem at *Cooks'n Corks* in Coquitlam, Brent & Robbin at *Kitchen Therapy* in South Surrey, and Karen Massier at the *UFV Campus* in Chilliwack.

Gratitude to all of the venues I have performed shows at over the past three years: West Coast Women's Show, Ridge Meadows Home Show, Chilliwack Fair, Abbotsford Learning Plus, Limbert Mountain Farm, Fraser Valley Retirement & Healthy Living Show, Milner Gardens, and especially the Abbotsford Agrifair where I perform 15 shows every year during the August long weekend and have been doing so for the past 9 years.

A great appreciation also to the following: Hendrix Restaurant Equipment & Supply, Jack & Debbie at JD Farms Specialty Turkey, Jerry & Audrey at Gelderman Farms, Frank Born at Born 3 Eggs, Ken & Don at Jackson Grills, Trafford Publishing, Wendy Gilmour of Gilmour Promotions, Aunty Dixie for her famous Baked Beans recipe, Bev & Sam, Bill Androsiuk, Simon Hill, The SHARE Imagine Gala, Fissler USA, Gary & Lisa Moran, Roger & Tracey Jamieson, Tina Bacon, Tasha Nagy, the Coquitlam Farmer's Market, Country 107.1, Deb Verbonac of Adfarm, Elaine Shock of Shock Ink, Toby Keith, Gerry & Sheila Hill, Bourquin Printers, and all of the Editors and Publishers of *Chef Dez on Cooking* for the ongoing support they have given me.

Lastly, I want to thank everyone who has attended my classes, welcomed me into their homes, attended my cooking shows, bought my first two books, and has been a dedicated reader of my columns. Without you . . . none of this would be a reality. Thank you all so much.

Table of Contents

The dream to open Lepp Farm Market in November, 2009, included offering regular evening cooking classes in our kitchen studio. Fraser Valley's Chef Dez was at the top of the list of potential instructors. Having read his regular newspaper column, I knew he was one who shared my passionate belief that enjoying top-quality home-cooked food with family and friends is one of life's greatest pleasures. To my delight, Chef Dez proposed writing a "Recipe of the Month" exclusively for Lepp Farm Market! From that partnership have emerged countless delicious recipes that marry his precise recipe writing and love of locally inspired dishes with Lepp's own premium products, and they are all graciously shared with you in this volume. From the first shared moment, as he prepared Warm Bacon Dressing in our kitchen, I knew I had found a local-food-loving kindred spirit!

"A smiling face is half the meal", says an old Latin Proverb. This exemplifies the spirit of Chef Dez's cooking shows. His "are we having fun yet?" shout at the start of each class reminds his "students" that food is meant to be enjoyed, and not taken too seriously. The detailed instructions, interspersed with stories about his own cooking mishaps, put everyone at ease: a perfect environment for the mostly sold-out classes to improve and hone their own cooking skills.

It's probably Chef Dez's accounting background that spurs him to perfect his recipes down to the smallest pinch of ingredients. While TV chefs spontaneously toss in this or that ingredient, it's precisely that technique which frustrates the home chef who wants to be able to rely on a recipe to recreate the same delicious results—exactly as presented, each and every time. Chef Dez's attention to detail, along with his culinary creativity, means that his recipes are consistently accurate. Not only that, they are simple enough for even a novice cook, guaranteed to produce gourmet dishes that leave dinner guests impressed.

As one with a bookcase of cookbooks, I know that, ultimately, the always-urgent "what's for dinner?" will find its answer in only a handful of cook books, food-splattered from regular use. *Chef Dez On Cooking Volume I and II* are included among those, so I'm beyond excited to add Volume III to the shelf! Congratulations, Dez, on your most recent accomplishment. Thank you, thank you, for helping all of us WOW our friends and loved ones with culinary delights.

And yes, we are having fun!
Charlotte Lepp,
Lepp Farm Market
Abbotsford, BC
leppfarmmarket.com

1

Garlic & Lemon Juice in Greek Cooking

Of my cooking classes, Greek are the most popular by far and this stems from my own passion for the flavours of Greece. Almost everyone I talk to loves Greek food and has frequented their local Greek Restaurants many times. People are always quick to mention their favourite ones and the best dishes that are served there.

I joke with people all the time that to create Greek food one basically adds olive oil, garlic, lemon juice, and oregano to anything and its Greek. Although these may be common denominators in many Greek recipes, there's a bit more to it than that to make good Greek food.

The most important thing to remember is ingredients from the source will always taste better in the final dish. Two ingredients that always come to mind when discussing this are garlic and lemon juice.

Garlic should never come from a jar. I see people in stores buying these large jars of peeled, chopped garlic in brine and I question it. The response is usually "it's cheap and convenient". Sounds like 'fast food' to me. Just because something is cheap and convenient, doesn't mean we should use it. Take any fresh cut vegetable (or fruit for that matter) and soak it in a jar full of brine—where does the flavour go? It leaches into the brine. So people who take a slotted spoon and add some of this garlic to a dish and say "I'm cooking with Garlic"—I respond and say "No, you're cooking with a residual, that was once garlic, and now most of the natural flavour has gone into the brine—which you're going to dump down the drain in a year once you have gotten through that humungous jar".

Many people also willingly pass through the produce section, walking by the lemons, on their way to the juice aisle to grab a bottle of lemon juice . . . again for the same reason "cheap and convenient". If you go to a lemon orchard in Florida or Italy, there are not bottles hanging from the trees. A reconstituted juice from concentrate will not give you the same flavour as what's offered from a fresh lemon. Plus you have the added bonus of reaping the aromatic and colourful zest from the outer peel to utilize as an additional ingredient or beautiful garnish.

We have to remember that the term "cheap and convenient" is not a synonym for "flavour" and if you want your Greek food, or any food, to taste better you need to go to the source of the ingredient you are adding for optimal results.

As a bonus I have included my recipe for Greek Salad. Enjoy!

Greek Salad

2 long English cucumbers, diced large
6-8 Roma tomatoes, diced large
1 large yellow pepper, diced large
1 large orange pepper, diced large
1 medium to large red onion, diced large
1 cup Kalamata olives
Dressing
1 cup olive oil
1/4 cup fresh lemon juice
3 tbsp red wine vinegar
2 tbsp dried oregano leaves
2 garlic cloves, crushed

2 tbsp sugar
salt and coarsely ground pepper to season
Crumbled feta cheese to garnish

1. In a large bowl, toss the vegetables and olives together.
2. In a separate bowl, mix the dressing ingredients well and pour over the salad. Toss to coat.
3. Garnish with crumbled feta cheese and season to taste with salt and pepper.

Broiled Greek Tomatoes

Full colour photo available at www.chefdez.com

12 medium Roma tomatoes, room temperature
Salt & freshly cracked pepper
1/3 cup finely chopped fresh oregano
Extra virgin olive oil
150g-200g crumbled feta cheese

1. Slice the tomatoes lengthwise (from core to bottom) into halves. Place the 24 halves, cut side up on a baking sheet (line with parchment for easy clean up).
2. Season liberally with salt and fresh cracked pepper.
3. Distribute the amount of chopped oregano evenly on the tomatoes.
4. Drizzle a small amount of olive oil on each tomato.
5. Distribute the feta cheese evenly on the tomatoes. *Tip—hold each tomato half over the cheese bowl to catch any cheese that falls off, and then return them to the baking sheet.
6. Broil under a hot preheated broiler for approximately 4 to 5 minutes until the cheese is slightly browned.

Makes 24 halves

Greek Lamb Burgers

Originally prepared for Lepp Farm Market www.leppfarmmarket.com
Full colour photo available at www.chefdez.com

"Cook until the burgers have reached 160 degrees Fahrenheit"

500g lean ground lamb
1 large egg
7 garlic cloves, crushed
3 tbsp finely chopped fresh oregano
2 tbsp finely chopped fresh rosemary
1 tsp salt
1/2 tsp pepper
100g feta cheese, crumbled

1. Mix all ingredients in a bowl and divide equally into four portions. Shape each portion into a burger patty.
2. On a preheated BBQ, grill the burgers over medium flame until cooked through or alternatively in a preheated pan over medium heat. Approximately 4 to 5 minutes per side but an instant read thermometer is the way to go: 71 degrees C or 160 degrees F.
3. Serve with Tzatziki, and lettuce, and optional tomato on your favourite burger buns.

Makes 4 burgers

Greek Tzatziki

"Do not peel the cucumbers, as the skin adds a lot of colour"

1 long English cucumber, grated
500g plain yogurt
3-4 garlic cloves, crushed
1 tbsp finely chopped fresh dill
1 tbsp olive oil
Salt and pepper to season

1. Put grated cucumbers in a clean towel or cheesecloth and squeeze to remove moisture.
2. Place drained cucumbers in a bowl, and add all the other ingredients; stir to combine.
3. Cover with plastic wrap and refrigerate for a minimum of two hours for the flavours to marry.

Makes approximately 3 cups

Greek Lemon Soup (Avgolemono)

"The classic name of this soup is Avgolemono from the ingredients eggs (avgo) and lemon juice (lemoni)"

8 cups chicken broth
1 cup long grain rice
1/2 tsp salt
4 large eggs
3/4 cup fresh lemon juice (approx 2-3 large lemons)
1 tsp sugar
Reserved zest from lemons

Chopped fresh parsley

1. In a large saucepan over high heat, bring the chicken broth to a boil.
2. Stir in the rice and the salt. Cover, reduce the heat to low and simmer for 20 minutes.
3. Separate the egg yolks from the egg whites.
4. About 5 minutes before the rice is done cooking in the broth, beat the yolks together in a small bowl, while in a large bowl whisk the egg whites until stiff peaks have formed. Slowly beat the mixed yolks into the whites. Then gradually beat the lemon juice into this egg mixture.
5. Gradually add 2 cups of the hot broth/rice mixture into the egg/juice mixture while whisking continuously. If the hot stock is added too fast, the eggs will curdle.
6. Once the 2 cups of broth has been added, stir the egg mixture into the large saucepan with the remaining broth/rice. Season with 1 teaspoon of sugar and serve immediately, garnished with the lemon zest and a small amount of chopped parsley.

Makes approximately 10.5 cups

Greek Rubbed Chicken

Originally prepared for Lepp Farm Market www.leppfarmmarket.com
Full colour photo available at www.chefdez.com

4 tsp dried oregano leaves
4 tsp granulated onion
4 tsp granulated garlic
4 tsp dried parsley
4 tsp dried rosemary
4 tsp sugar
2 tsp cornstarch

2 tsp salt

2 tsp ground pepper

Zest from 2 lemons, finely grated or chopped

8 bone-in pieces of chicken

Olive oil

Juice from 1/2 lemon

1. Preheat the oven to 400 degrees Fahrenheit.
2. In a small bowl combine the oregano, onion, garlic, parsley, rosemary, sugar, salt, pepper, cornstarch, and lemon zest to form a dry rub. Set aside.
3. Rub the chicken pieces on both sides with some olive oil. Dredge the chicken pieces in the dry rub from step number 2, making sure it is applied to all areas and crevices of the chicken.
4. Place the chicken, skin side up, on a rack on a baking pan. Bake in the oven for approximately 40 minutes until an instant read thermometer, in the thickest parts of the pieces, reads 165 degrees Fahrenheit.
5. Remove from the oven and immediately squeeze the half lemon over the chicken.

Makes 8 portions

Pastitsio

Full colour photo available at www.chefdez.com

"A Greek baked pasta dish at its finest"

1 pound lean ground beef

1 large onion, diced small, approximately 2 cups

4 to 6 garlic cloves, minced

1 tbsp dried oregano

2 to 3 tsp salt

1 tsp pepper

1-156ml can tomato paste

1-796ml can of diced tomatoes

1 & 1/2 cups full bodied red wine

2 bay leaves

5 tbsp butter

6 tbsp flour

3 cups milk

1 tsp salt

1/4 tsp pepper

1/4 tsp ground nutmeg

2 cups crumbled feta cheese

500g macaroni type pasta

3 large eggs

1. Preheat the oven to 350 degrees Fahrenheit and prepare a 9 x 13 x 2.5 inch baking pan with baking spray.

2. Brown the beef in a large pan over medium heat. Stir in the onion, garlic, oregano, 2 tsp of the salt, and the pepper. Cook until the onion and garlic are soft, approximately 2 to 3 minutes.

3. Stir in the tomato paste, tomatoes, wine, and bay leaves. Bring to a boil and then simmer until sauce consistency is reached, approximately 10 minutes. Season with the other tsp of salt if desired, and set aside.

4. In a separate pot melt the butter over low heat. Stir in the flour and cook for approximately 5 minutes, stirring occasionally (this removes the starchy taste of the flour). Add the milk gradually, while whisking constantly, until all the milk has been thoroughly incorporated. Stir in the 1 tsp salt, 1/4 tsp pepper, and 1/4 tsp nutmeg. Bring to boil over medium heat, while stirring occasionally, to thicken this white sauce. Stir in 1 cup of the crumbled feta cheese and set aside.

5. Cook your pasta to desired consistency.

6. In a mixing bowl beat the eggs. Gradually add a small amount (approximately 1/3) of your reserved white sauce into the eggs while whisking constantly—this will temper the eggs to come up in temperature gradually without curdling them. Then mix this tempered egg/sauce mixture back into the remaining white sauce.

7. Assemble your pan as follows: one layer of half of the pasta, top with the remaining cup of crumbled feta cheese, top with the meat sauce, top with the remaining pasta, and finally top with the white sauce.

8. Bake in the oven for approximately 30 minutes to set the eggs in the white sauce. Then broil until lightly browned. Let rest for 10 to 15 minutes before cutting as desired, and serve.

Makes 9 large portions or 12 smaller portions

Stewed Leg of Lamb

3 to 4 pound boneless leg of lamb
3 tbsp grape seed oil or canola oil
Salt & pepper
1/2 cup beef broth
1 small/medium carrot, diced small
1 stalk of celery, diced small
1 medium onion, diced small
8 cloves garlic, minced
1 tsp salt
1-796ml can diced tomatoes
1 cup red wine
3 to 4 tbsp chopped fresh rosemary
2 bay leaves
2 tbsp sugar
3 to 4 tbsp chopped fresh oregano
Salt & pepper to taste, if needed

1. Cut the lamb into 4 to 5 large pieces, coat with 2 tbsp of the oil and season with salt and pepper.

2. Preheat a large heavy bottomed pan over medium-high heat. When hot, add the other 1 tbsp of oil and immediately sear each piece of lamb on all sides until browned—only searing enough pieces at one time so that you don't crowd the pan. Remove and set aside.

3. Carefully deglaze the pan with the beef broth and then add the carrot, celery, onion, garlic, and salt. Cook for 2 to 3 minutes until soft.

4. Add the tomatoes, wine, rosemary, bay leaves, and the lamb to the pan. Bring to a boil and then cover and reduce the heat to low and simmer for 90 minutes, turning the lamb pieces over halfway through this cooking process.

5. After the 90 minute cooking time remove the lamb and set aside, tenting with foil to keep warm. Turn the heat to medium/high to high and boil to reduce the liquid until desired sauce consistency has been reached.

6. Remove from the heat. Remove and discard the bay leaves.

7. Stir in the sugar and fresh oregano. Taste and season with salt and pepper if desired. Cut the lamb into smaller desired chunks and stir back into the sauce. Serve immediately.

Makes approximately 6 to 8 portions

2

Expand Culinary Knowledge within Your Budget

Economic focus is in the news more than ever these days, and everyone seems like they're searching for ways to tighten their purse strings. There are ways however, to expand your knowledge in the culinary world without affecting your personal/family grocery budget. Let's face it, we all need to eat food to stay alive, and adding some variety to our home meals is a way to make "eating in" more exciting.

How many times has the normal trip to the grocery supermarket resulted in bringing home the same old products that you always buy, for your never changing home menu? This can very easily be changed without any drastic affect on your monthly food budget.

Here's what I want you to do: every week, two weeks, or month, I want you to buy just one product you would never normally buy. This could be a produce item, a spice, an herb, or something down the imported food aisle. Take your blinders off, step outside your habitual boundaries, and be receptive to all the wonderful products we have available at our finger tips. No matter where you live, shopping today has a greater abundance of selection than ever before.

The other great resource we have access to, whether it's at home, work or the local libraries, is the internet. This will allow you to answer questions about the certain product that you have purchased that you may know nothing about. What do I do with it? How do I prepare it? How is it normally served? How is it best stored?

You and your family are going to be eating food anyway, and chances are you will continue to do so the rest of your life. What harm will it be then to spend, for example, two or three dollars per month on one product you normally wouldn't purchase? Continue to do this for a year, while researching and educating yourself on each product and you will have expanded your culinary knowledge by twelve items. This will add variety to your home menu forever and at the same time build your culinary knowledge.

Many cities/towns also have gourmet food stores. Make it a habit to talk to these people, tap into their expertise, and make your weekly/monthly one product purchase there instead of, or alternating with, your regular grocery store.

If you have even more room in your monthly budget, take a cooking class once per month instead of dining out. I know my restaurant friends will dislike me saying so, but the return on your investment in a cooking class is far greater than just a full stomach from one "dining out" visit. As the old saying goes "give a person a fish and you will feed them for a day; teach them to fish and you feed them for life".

Dear Chef Dez:
    I like onions and someone suggested trying shallots. What is the difference between onions and shallots and why are shallots are so much more expensive?

                Harry N.
                Yorkton, SK

Dear Harry:
    Shallots are a relative of the onion and basically are milder and sweeter than regular cooking onions, and thus tend not to overpower other flavours. They are so expensive mainly because of supply/demand. In my hometown onions are usually priced at about 60-75 cents per pound, while shallots are 3 dollars per pound. If there was a gradual increase in the demand of shallots, the cultivation of these root vegetables would be increased and the price would eventually start falling. I am not a gardener by any means, but from what I understand shallots can be successfully produced wherever onions are grown.

Chick Pea Curry

Full colour photo available at www.chefdez.com

2 tbsp canola oil
1 small onion, diced small
1 carrot, 1/4'd and sliced thin
1 celery stalk, 1/2'd and sliced thin
4 garlic cloves, minced
2 tbsp dark brown sugar
1 tbsp salt
1 tbsp curry powder
2 tsp garam masala
1 tsp turmeric
1/2 tsp pepper
1 - 540ml can chick peas, drained, reserving 2 tbsp liquid
1 red bell pepper, diced small
1-398ml can coconut milk
1 tsp vegetable paste
2 tbsp cornstarch dissolved in the reserved chick pea liquid
Cooked chicken or cooked prawns, optional
Garnish with plain yogurt, currants, and chopped cilantro

1. Heat a large pan slightly over medium heat. Add the oil, onion, carrot, celery, garlic, sugar, salt, curry powder, garam masala, turmeric, and pepper. Mix together and cook for approximately 5 minutes, stirring occasionally, until vegetables are soft and the mixture becomes thick.
2. Add the drained chick peas, bell pepper, coconut milk, vegetable paste, and dissolved cornstarch mixture. Heat to a boil while stirring to thicken.
3. *Optional—stir in cooked chicken or cooked prawns.
4. Serve immediately garnished with plain yogurt, currants, and cilantro

Makes approximately 4 portions

Chicken & Sausage Gumbo

"Constant stirring of the roux (fat & flour) will help prevent it from burning. My version of a gumbo thickened with both roux and okra. The amount of salt you use will depend on how salty your chicken broth is."

1/2 cup canola oil or vegetable oil
1/2 cup flour
1 medium onion, diced small, approximately 1.5 cups
1 medium red bell pepper, diced small, approximately 1 cup
2 celery stalks, diced small, approximately 1 cup
1-300g package frozen okra, thawed & sliced into circles
2 tsp dried thyme leaves (not ground)
2 bay leaves
6 to 8 garlic cloves, chopped
454g smoked andouille sausage, sliced lengthwise in half, then sliced into small pieces
10 boneless/skinless chicken thighs, cut into bite sized chunks
1/2 cup white wine
4 cups chicken broth
3 tsp sugar
1-156ml can tomato paste
1/2 tsp pepper
1 to 2 tsp salt, to taste
Cooked rice

1. Heat a large heavy bottomed pot over medium-high heat. Add the oil and heat slightly. Stir in the flour and reduce the heat to medium or medium-low and stir constantly for 20-30 minutes until this mixture (called a roux, pronounced 'roo') has turned dark brown, resembling the colour of melted milk chocolate.
2. Stir in the onion, bell pepper, and celery. Turn up the heat to medium and cook for approximately 2 to 3 minutes, stirring occasionally. It will get extremely thick.
3. Stir in the okra, thyme, and bay leaves and cook for approximately 2 to 3 more minutes, stirring occasionally.

4. Stir in the garlic, sausage, chicken, and wine. Cook for 5 minutes, stirring constantly until the chicken has mostly cooked.
5. Stir in the broth, sugar, tomato paste, and pepper. Increase the heat to high and bring to a boil. Then simmer at a low boil, uncovered, for 30 minutes, stirring occasionally, until it has reduced and thickened.
6. Season to taste with the salt and serve immediately over cooked rice.

Makes 6 to 8 portions

Creole Halibut BBQ Pouches

Originally prepared for Lepp Farm Market www.leppfarmmarket.com
Full colour photo available at www.chefdez.com

"The holy trinity of bell pepper, celery & onion; along with garlic, tomatoes, thyme, sweet smoked paprika and cayenne, give this seafood dish delicious Creole flavour"

4 halibut filets, approx. 200-250g each
Salt & pepper
12 cherry tomatoes, quartered
1 stalk celery, sliced thin
1 small yellow bell pepper, cut into small short strips
4 garlic cloves, minced
8 thin slices onion
12 fresh thyme sprigs
2 tsp smoked sweet paprika
Ground cayenne pepper, optional
1 tsp sugar
4 tbsp cold butter
1 lemon

1. Preheat BBQ grill with high heat.

2.   Cut 8 pieces of heavy duty aluminum foil—12 inches x 18 inches. Lay 2 pieces of foil on top of each other to make 4 separate double-layer foil bases.

3.   Place each filet, skin side down, in the center of one half of each of the foil bases, and season each filet liberally with salt and pepper.

4.   Top each filet evenly with 3 quartered tomatoes, equal amounts of celery, equal amounts of bell pepper, 1 minced garlic clove, 2 thin slices of onion, 3 sprigs of thyme, 1/2 tsp paprika, pinch of cayenne, 1/4 tsp sugar, and season with more salt & pepper.

5.   Top each mound with a 1 tbsp pat of butter.

6.   Seal the pouches by folding over the foil in half longwise over the vegetable covered fish. Starting at one end, fold in and crimp the edges of the foil tightly and work around the whole open side of the foil to form a semi-circle pouch. It must be tightly sealed to keep all the steam and juices in the pouch.

7.   Place the pouches on the hot BBQ grill and reduce heat to medium low. Close the lid and cook for approximately 12 to 15 minutes while trying to maintain a cooking temperature of 375 degrees F on your BBQ's built-in gauge.

8.   Remove pouches from the grill and let sit for 5 minutes before opening. The internal temperature of the fish should be 140-150 degrees F.

9.   Cut open each pouch, squeeze over a bit of fresh lemon juice, and serve immediately.

Makes 4 portions

*Alternatively you can cook these pouches in the oven at 450-475 degrees F for 12 to 15 minutes.

Fillets of Sole Meuniere

"Pronounced 'mun yair,' this is a classic fish preparation"

Canola oil
6 sole fillets (approx. 60g each)
Salt & pepper
Flour
Juice of a lemon, approx. 2 tbsp
1/4 cup chopped parsley
5 tbsp butter

1. Heat a non-stick pan over medium-high heat.
2. While heating, season the fillets with salt & pepper, then dredge in flour.
3. Add approximately 1 tbsp canola oil to the pan and then add the fillets to the pan, presentation side down first. Sauté until lightly browned. Turn over carefully with a spatula and brown the other side.
4. Transfer the fillets to plates and squeeze the lemon over them. Sprinkle with parsley.
5. Add the butter to the hot pan and swirl until foaming brown to make browned butter and immediately pour it over the fish.

Makes 6 portions

Mexican Mole Sauce for Chicken

"Big bold flavour with smoky heat, finished with unsweetened chocolate"

1 tbsp cumin seed
2 inch stick of cinnamon
2 dry bay leaves
1 tbsp dry oregano leaves
2 tbsp canola oil
1/3 cup peanuts
1/3 cup slivered almonds
1/3 cup raisins
1 medium onion, chopped
6 garlic cloves, chopped
2 tsp salt
1/2 tsp pepper
2 to 3 canned chipotle peppers
1-796ml can diced tomatoes, drained well
2oz. unsweetened chocolate, chopped
2 cups chicken broth
1/4 cup dark brown sugar
Juice of 1 lime
Cooked chicken
Cooked rice
Sour cream, optional
Chopped fresh cilantro, optional

1. Heat cumin seeds and cinnamon stick in a large pan over medium heat until the seeds start to smoke and become fragrant, approximately 3 to 4 minutes. Transfer to a spice grinder with the bay leaves and oregano and process until fully ground. Set aside.

2. Return the pan to the heat until hot. Add the oil and fry the peanuts and almonds until coloured, approximately 1 to 2 minutes. BE CAREFUL NOT TO BURN THEM. Remove with a slotted spoon and set aside.

3. Return the oiled pan to the heat, add the raisins and fry them for approximately 30 seconds until they are plump. BE CAREFUL NOT TO BURN THEM. Remove with a slotted spoon and set aside with the nuts.

4. Return the pan to the heat. Add the onion, garlic, salt and pepper. Cook until the onion just starts to caramelize, approximately 1 to 2 minutes. Then add the chipotle peppers and the drained tomatoes and cook for 2 minutes more.

5. Add all of the above (ground spices, peanuts, almonds, raisins, onion, garlic, chipotles, and tomatoes) to a blender or food processor. Add 1 cup of the chicken broth and process until smooth. *Optional—pass through a strainer after pureeing for a completely smooth consistency.

6. Add this pureed sauce back to the pan over medium heat. Add the chocolate, the other cup of chicken broth, and the brown sugar. Heat until the chocolate has melted and the sauce is hot.

7. Remove the pan from the heat and stir in the lime juice. Season to taste with salt and pepper and serve over cooked chicken and rice. Top each portion with a dollop of sour cream and a sprinkle of chopped cilantro, optional.

Makes 5 cups of sauce

Pear & Cappicollo Antipasti

"A wonderful appetizer of contrasting flavours with a beautiful display on the plate"

2 pears, cored, quartered & sliced thin
2 tbsp lemon juice
1 tbsp water
250g mild capicollo, shaved
75g Gorgonzola cheese

3 tbsp whipping cream
3/4 cup pecan halves, toasted

1. Toss the pear slices in mixture of lemon juice and water, to prevent oxidization.
2. Arrange the pear slices in circular designs on 4 small plates, with points towards the outside of the plates.
3. Divide and arrange the capicollo in the middle of the 4 pear displays.
4. Cut or break the Gorgonzola into pieces. Place with the cream in a stainless steel bowl. Place over a pot of simmering water and stir until the cheese has melted and combined with the cream. Remove from the heat and let stand 2-3 minutes to cool slightly and thicken.
5. Drizzle the Gorgonzola cream over the capicollo and pears. Garnish with the toasted pecans and serve immediately.

Makes 4 portions

3

Helping You Bring Dinner to the Table More Easily

The start of a new school year is always a bit of an adjustment in our time schedules from the lazy, hazy days of summer. Even people who are not parents are impacted by longer commuting times due to the increased traffic on the roads. Having some quick and easy meal ideas in our home menu repertoires can make a world of difference when it come to the stress level of preparing dinner.

Our society is bombarded with artificial solutions to our hectic lives, such as fast food restaurants and premade, prepackaged meals. It is a sad state of reality when quick and nutritious meals are only an idea away. Yes, some planning needs to be involved, but it is not as difficult as one may first think.

Slow cookers are the most obvious answer and many recipes can be found at your local library or on the internet. I was astounded when I first saw a commercial recently that advertised a prepackaged slow-cooker meal: one that is easily emptied from the bag frozen into your crock pot. Yes, this is still better than deep fried fast-food, but it is basic cooking and not only is it costing you a fortune in comparison to making it yourself, you also have no control of any preservatives that may be included.

Casseroles are another resolution and very popular with kids. Again this requires some planning, but the most time efficient method would be to prepare two or three casseroles of the same dish at once. This would allow you to freeze the extra meals for an even quicker solution to your busiest evenings. Other dishes that could fall under this same category would be meatloaves, lasagna, shepherd's pies, cabbage rolls, etc. For dishes like this that are to be made in abundance and kept frozen, find the day of the week that works best for you, like a Sunday afternoon for example.

There are many other non-casserole recipes that can be prepared ahead of time as well like pasta sauces, pizzas, stir frys, etc. Food is not only an avenue to keep us alive, but it is an opportunity to celebrate life, nutrition, and the joys of flavours.

Unfortunately in today's society, many people don't see the appeal in bringing the family meal together, and have classified cooking as a household chore. A more accurate example of a household chore would be vacuuming, not cooking. How many times have you called up a friend and asked if they want to vacuum with you? Probably never. Such gatherings are almost always over dinner, lunch or coffee and a treat. Food is life in so many ways; nutrition, building relationships, pleasure from flavours, etc, and the first thing we need to change is our vision when it comes to food and cooking.

Look for the negatives in anything and you will find them. Look for the positives and your perception will change. Yes, my opinion is obviously biased, but what would you rather do: have pride in making (and eating) a great meal, or clean your carpet?

Dear Chef Dez:

I like the taste of garlic in different dishes, however when I add it to a stir-fry it always adds a bitter flavour. What am I doing wrong?

Sincerely,
John D.
Abbotsford, BC

Dear John:

If this is the only time you experience a bitter flavour from the addition of garlic to a recipe, I suspect that it is getting burned. Garlic burns very easily, especially if added to the extreme temperature of oil in "wok cooking". To avoid this problem in the future, always add a different vegetable first to the hot oil to temper it a little before adding the garlic.

Beef & Black Bean Enchiladas

Originally prepared for Lepp Farm Market www.leppfarmmarket.com
Full colour photo available at www.chefdez.com

1.5 pounds (680g) lean ground beef
1 cup small diced onion
6 to 8 garlic cloves, minced
2 tbsp Mexican chilli powder
1 tbsp dried oregano
1 tbsp dried ground cumin
2 tsp salt
½ tsp pepper
3 tbsp canned green chillies
2 tbsp dark brown sugar
2 cups canned crushed tomatoes
1-398ml can black beans, rinsed & drained
6 large soft flour tortillas
340g old cheddar, grated
Toppings:
Sour cream
Sliced canned black olives, drained
Small diced fresh tomatoes
Green onions, sliced

1. Preheat oven to 350 degrees Fahrenheit and prepare a 9x13 pan with baking spray.
2. Brown the beef in a large frying pan over medium to medium-high heat.
3. Add the diced onion, garlic, chilli powder, oregano, cumin, salt, pepper, green chillies, brown sugar and 1 cup of the crushed tomatoes. Stir to combine and cook for approximately 2 to 3 minutes, over medium heat, until the onions are softened.
4. Remove 1 cup of this cooked meat sauce and in a small bowl mix it with the second cup of crushed tomatoes—set aside.

5. Stir in the black beans to the remaining meat sauce in the pan and remove from the heat.

6. Set out the 6 tortillas on the counter and equally spoon out all of the meat/bean mixture onto them.

7. Spread 1 cup of the reserved meat/tomato mixture into the prepared 9x13 pan.

8. Roll up each tortilla and place them in the pan (seam side down) one at a time, until all 6 are in the pan.

9. Spread the remaining reserved meat/tomato mixture down the centre on the enchiladas and top evenly with the grated cheese.

10. Bake for 30 minutes until hot and the cheese has melted/browned.

11. Top with sour cream, black olives, tomatoes and green onions, either while still in the pan or individually.

Makes 6 Portions

Beef Barley Slow-Cooker Stew

Originally prepared for Lepp Farm Market www.leppfarmmarket.com
Full colour photo available at www.chefdez.com

"Beef stock paste is a reduction of beef juices to paste form, and used instead of bouillon cubes. Traditionally 1 tsp of this paste mixed with 1 cup of water would make 1 cup of broth. I use apple cider, and the juice from the tomatoes, in this recipe instead of water because water has no flavour."

680g (1.5 pounds) beef stew meat
3 tbsp canola oil
Salt & pepper
2 medium onions, chopped
1 large carrot, sliced lengthwise, then ½ inch pieces
2 celery stalks, sliced ½ inch pieces
8 to 10 garlic cloves
3 tbsp apple cider

8 medium mushrooms, quartered
2 to 3 tbsp chopped fresh rosemary
2 bay leaves
2 tsp beef stock paste
1/2 cup pearl barley
1-798ml can diced tomatoes
2 cups apple cider

1. Preheat a large pan over medium-high heat. In a bowl toss beef pieces with 2 tablespoons of oil and season with salt and pepper. When the pan is hot, add the other tablespoon of oil to the pan and brown each piece of meat without crowding the pan—you may have to brown the beef in 2 or 3 batches. When each batch of meat is browned transfer to the slow-cooker.
2. Turn off the heat to the pan and add the onions, carrot, celery, garlic and the 3 tablespoons of apple cider to the pan. Stir until the pan has cooled and the vegetables have cooked slightly, approximately 1 to 2 minutes. Transfer this vegetable mixture to the slow-cooker.
3. To the slow-cooker add the mushrooms, rosemary, bay leaves, beef paste, barley, tomatoes (with juice) and the apple cider.
4. Turn the slow-cooker on low and cook for approximately 8 to 10 hours.
5. Remove and discard the bay leaves and season to taste with salt and pepper before serving.

Makes approximately 12 cups

Butternut Squash & Coconut Soup

"A great vegetarian soup!"

1 tbsp olive oil
1 medium onion, diced small
4-5cm long piece of ginger, peeled and cut in fine strips
1 butternut squash (about 1 kilo), peeled and cut in 1/2 inch cubes
4 cups vegetable stock
1-400ml can of coconut milk
Salt & pepper to taste
Toasted pumpkin seeds
Fresh cilantro

1. Heat the olive oil in a large pan over medium heat, add the onion and ginger and cook until soft, approximately 2 to 3 minutes. Add the butternut squash and cook for about 2-3 more minutes. Then add the stock and bring to a boil over high heat. Reduce the heat and simmer for about 20 minutes until butternut squash is soft.
2. Add the coconut milk and puree with a handheld mixer until you get a very smooth soup. Season with salt and fresh cracked pepper to taste. Serve immediately garnished with toasted pumpkin seeds and fresh cilantro.

Makes approximately 8 cups

Mexican Casserole

Full colour photo available at www.chefdez.com

1 & 1/2 pounds (680g) lean ground beef
1 cup small diced onion
6 to 8 garlic cloves, minced

2 tbsp Mexican chilli powder

1 tbsp dried oregano

1 tbsp dried ground cumin

2 tsp salt

1/2 tsp pepper

3 tbsp canned green chillies

2 tbsp dark brown sugar

1 cup canned crushed tomatoes

1-398ml can refried beans

2 cups cooked rice

1-398ml can black beans, rinsed & drained

340g old cheddar, grated

Toppings:

Sour cream

Sliced canned black olives, drained

Small diced fresh tomatoes

Green onions, sliced

1. Preheat oven to 350 degrees Fahrenheit and prepare a 9x13 pan with baking spray.
2. Brown the beef in a large frying pan over medium to medium-high heat.
3. Add the diced onion, garlic, chilli powder, oregano, cumin, salt, pepper, green chillies, brown sugar and the crushed tomatoes. Stir to combine and cook for approximately 2 to 3 minutes, over medium heat, until the onions are softened. Remove from the heat and set aside.
4. In the prepared 9x13 pan, spread the refried beans evenly to form the base layer of the casserole. On top of this refried bean layer, continue evenly building the casserole with these layers in the following order: cooked rice, reserved meat sauce, black beans, and finally the grated cheddar.
5. Bake for 20 minutes and then top with some crumbled tortilla chips. Continue to bake for 10 more minutes until hot and the cheese has melted/browned.
6. Top with sour cream, black olives, tomatoes and green onions, either while still in the pan or individually.

Makes 8 to 12 portions

Pot Roast with Wild Mushroom Gravy

Originally prepared for Lepp Farm Market www.leppfarmmarket.com
Full colour photo available at www.chefdez.com

One 3 pound cross rib pot roast—or—chuck pot roast
Salt & Pepper
1 to 2 tbsp grape seed oil or canola oil
1/2 cup red wine
1 small onion, chopped
1 celery stalk, sliced
1 medium carrot, sliced
6 whole garlic cloves, peeled
20g dried wild mushrooms
2 cups beef broth
More broth as needed
1 tsp sugar
Salt & pepper to taste

1. Preheat oven to 325 degrees F.
2. Heat a cast iron pot, or enamel coated cast iron pot, over medium high heat. While waiting for the pot to heat, liberally salt & pepper the roast.
3. Once the pot is hot, add the oil and immediately start searing all sides of the roast until browned.
4. Once all sides are browned, remove the roast and set aside temporarily.
5. Turn off the burner heat and once the pot has cooled slightly, carefully deglaze with the red wine (this removes the browned bits (fond) from the bottom of the pot into the wine). Add the onion, celery, carrot, garlic and dried mushrooms. Stir to coat.
6. Add the beef broth and the roast. Cover and cook for 2 hours and 15 minutes.
7. Carefully remove the roast and set aside while preparing the gravy.
8. Remove the rehydrated mushrooms and chop finely and set aside.

9. Puree the remaining ingredients in the pot until smooth while adding additional broth to make desired consistency—a power hand blender is ideal for this, or you can transfer to a food processor and then transfer back to the pot.
10. Add the chopped mushrooms and put the pot on medium or medium/high heat to heat the gravy thoroughly. Season to taste with the sugar and salt & pepper, and serve immediately.

Makes approximately 4 to 6 portions

Note: If making a roast of a different size (weight), then I would approximate the cooking time at 45 minutes per pound in a 325 degree Fahrenheit oven. Please keep in mind however, the larger the roast, the more broth and vegetables should be added for adequate cooking liquid and ample gravy and flavour when finished. Pureeing the vegetables into the gravy makes not only complex tasting gravy, but also eliminates the need for a starch thickener.

Slow-Cooker Pulled Pork

Full colour photo available at www.chefdez.com

"Great pulled pork sandwiches in the ease of a slow-cooker. Serve on buns topped with coleslaw and your favourite mustard."

2kg to 2.5kg boneless pork butt roast (pork shoulder roast)
2 tbsp canola oil
Salt & pepper

1 medium onion, sliced
8 garlic cloves, chopped
1/2 cup brown sugar (not golden sugar)
2 tbsp chilli powder
1 tbsp liquid smoke
4 tsp salt

1 tsp pepper
1/2 cup beef broth

1/3 cup brown sugar (not golden sugar)
1 tbsp white vinegar
1 tsp salt, or to taste
3 tbsp cornstarch dissolved in 3 tbsp beef broth or red wine

1. Cut the pork roast into 5 or 6 equal sized chunks. Coat with the canola oil and season with salt & pepper. Heat a pan over medium-high heat and once hot sear the chunks of pork until browned on all sides. Make sure you do not crowd the pan or they won't brown as well. As each chunk is seared, place in slow-cooker.
2. While the pork chunks are searing, add the onion, garlic, 1/2 cup brown sugar, chilli powder, liquid smoke, 4 tsp salt, and 1 tsp pepper to the slow-cooker.
3. When the pork is done searing and all chunks are now in the slow-cooker, carefully add the beef broth to the pan and stir to deglaze (remove the browned bits off the pan into the liquid). Now add this broth to the slow-cooker as well.
4. Put the lid on the slow cooker and turn on low. Cook for 8 to 9 hours.
5. Once cooked, remove the chunks of pork from the liquid. Shred each piece of pork with 2 forks and set aside in a covered large bowl to keep warm.
6. Pour the liquid (and chunks of garlic and garlic) into a pot. Puree with a hand immersion blender (or place in a food processor or blender to puree smooth, and then into a pot). Stir in the 1/3 cup brown sugar, white vinegar, salt, and the dissolved cornstarch. Bring to a boil to thicken. Mix in 3 cups of this thickened sauce to the shredded pork. (keep leftover sauce to serve as extra dipping sauce if desired)
7. Serve on buns topped with coleslaw and your favourite mustard.

Makes approximately 8 cups of pulled pork

Slow-Cooker Thai Squash Soup

Originally prepared for Lepp Farm Market www.leppfarmmarket.com
Full colour photo available at www.chefdez.com

"I have used a couple different kinds of squash for a more complex squash flavour. I am sure everyone is familiar with butternut squash, but how many of you have worked with a kabocha squash? Kabocha is hard, has knobbly-looking skin, is shaped like a squatty pumpkin, and has a dull finished deep green skin. It has an exceptional naturally sweet flavor, even sweeter than butternut, and has a similar flavour and texture to a pumpkin and sweet potato combined. If kabocha is not available, use acorn squash, or all butternut. If you want the soup spicier, then puree more of the red Thai curry paste in at the end."

1 medium onion, chopped
2-3 large garlic cloves, chopped
2 tbsp minced fresh ginger
3-4 tsp red Thai curry paste
3 tbsp sugar
1 tbsp salt
5 cups of 1/2 inch cubed, peeled, seeded kabocha squash
5 cups of 1/2 inch cubed, peeled, seeded butternut squash
2 cups chicken stock
1-400ml can of coconut milk
Juice of 1 lime
Salt & pepper to season
Optional garnish: Toasted sweet grated coconut, toasted pumpkin seeds, fresh cilantro

1. Add the onion, garlic, ginger, curry paste, sugar, salt, kabocha, butternut, chicken stock, and coconut milk (with the thick coconut cream on the surface of the canned milk) to a slow cooker. Stir thoroughly to combine.
2. Cook on low setting for 7 to 9 hours until the squash is tender.
3. Puree with a hand submersion blender (or food processor, or blender) until the texture is very smooth. Stir in the fresh lime juice and season to taste with salt and pepper, if desired. If the consistency is too thick add some more chicken stock.
4. Garnish each bowl and serve immediately.

Makes approximately 9 cups

4

All About
Flank Steak

Flank steak is one of my favourite cuts of beef for the BBQ because it has great flavour, and is extremely tender when cut and prepared properly. Due to the fact that there are many people that don't know much about this specific cut, it tends to be a very underrated steak in comparison to more popular cuts such as strip loin, sirloin, rib-eye, etc. There is also a lot of misinformation in the media about flank steak and I hope to clear up some of this confusion for you.

Beef flank steak is a long and flat cut of meat from the abdominal muscles of the cow. It is significantly tougher than other cuts of meat as it comes from a strong well-exercised part of the cow. The direction of the grain of the meat and connective tissue is prominently visible, especially in the raw form. Moist heat techniques, such as braising, will be successful in making the meat tender, but it can also be simply grilled to a rare/medium-rare/medium doneness and then sliced thinly across the grain, and still be very tender.

I have witnessed many Chefs on TV state that one must marinate a flank steak before grilling in order for it to be tender. This is not true. Although marinating is fine to do with a flank steak, it is an optional step, not a requirement. The acid in a marinade will break down the connective tissue over time, but I have BBQ'd so many flank steaks that have been "melt in your mouth" tender, with no marinating whatsoever. The secret is to make sure you don't over-cook the steak and then slice it thinly in the opposite direction of how the grain of the meat is running (across the grain).

For optimal flavour, my preferred way of preparing flank steak is to first coat it with a spice rub, grill it to the desired doneness, let it rest for a few minutes, slice it very thinly across the grain, and then drizzle it with garlic butter. When slicing it thinly, I also make sure I slice it on an angle, approximately 45 degrees. Flank steak is a very thin cut of meat and slicing it on a 45 degree angle will make more elongated slices and provide better plate coverage, or sandwich coverage.

Letting it rest after cooking will help the steak to retain more of its juices. All meat, from a small steak to large roasts or turkeys, should have a resting time for this reason. The bigger the size of the meat, the longer it should rest. I let a flank steak rest for at least 5 minutes.

I have also seen Chefs on TV take a knife and "score" the flank steak before going into their marinade—in my opinion this is incorrect as well. Although at first it may seem to make sense to put cuts into the surface of the meat to aid in the penetration of the marinade into the inside of the steak, however this goes against one of the golden rules of grilling meats: Never Pierce your Meat. The goal of cooking meat is to have the end result as a juicy flavourful product. If you pierce your meat (by jabbing a fork into it for flipping, or cutting into it), then valuable juices will be lost. Meat that has been scored prior to cooking will suffer the same damaging situation, and always use tongs to flip your steak, not a fork.

Many premade spice rubs for meat can be purchased at your local grocery store, but I find it more satisfying to create different ones myself with ingredients I have on hand already. Here is a basic Cajun blackening spice rub recipe for you to experiment with. If available in your area, try replacing the paprika (or at least a portion of it) with a sweet smoked paprika for more flavour. Happy cooking!

Cajun Blackening Spice Rub

"A perfect way to add tons of flavour. Store in an air-tight container for 3 to 6 months."

1-quarter cup paprika
2 tsp dried oregano
2 tsp ground black pepper
2 tsp salt
1 tsp dried thyme
1-half tsp cayenne pepper, or more if you like it hotter

1. Mix all ingredients together.
2. Use it to liberally coat beef, pork, poultry, or fish before grilling or pan-frying.
3. Finish cooked product with a drizzle of garlic butter.

Makes just over 1-quarter cup of spice

Beef Grilling Rub

"A great basic spice rub for all beef destined for the BBQ"

4 tbsp sweet smoked paprika
2 tbsp dried granulated garlic
4 tsp salt
2 tsp ground black pepper
2 tsp dried thyme leaves
1/2 tsp ground cayenne pepper, optional

1. Mix together and thoroughly coat your choice of beef before grilling.

Makes approximately 1/2 cup

Flambéed Mushrooms

"One of the easiest side dishes, or steak toppers, you will ever make—and a showy one at the stove or side burner of your BBQ!"

2 tbsp canola oil
1 pound (454g) button mushrooms, quartered
1/2 tsp dried thyme
Salt & pepper
1 tbsp Scotch whiskey

1. Heat a medium pan over medium-high heat.
2. Add the oil, then the mushrooms, thyme, and season with salt & pepper. Saute until the mushrooms have shrunk in size and they start to turn brown, approximately 5 to 7 minutes, stirring occasionally.
3. Remove the pan from the heat to let cool slightly, approximately 30 seconds. Carefully add the whiskey and carefully ignite with a long match/lighter. Flambé until the flames subside.
4. Re-season with salt & pepper if necessary, and serve immediately as a side dish or on top of steak.

Makes 4 side portions

Grilled Philly Cheesesteaks

Originally prepared for Lepp Farm Market www.leppfarmmarket.com
Full colour photo available at www.chefdez.com

"This grilled version of the classic Philly Cheesesteak has incredible "flame licked" flavour that would be non-existent in the traditional way of preparing it in a pan. I find the addition of mayonnaise is extremely important for not only adding richness, but also to help enhance the gooey drippy effect that a classic chees-esteak should have."

2 pounds (908g) rib-eye steaks
2 medium onions, sliced into 4 thick rounds each
2 red bell peppers, sliced into big pieces
Canola, vegetable or grape seed oil
Salt & pepper
1/2 cup butter
3 garlic cloves, finely minced
2 tbsp Worcestershire sauce
6 oval hoagie type buns
12 tbsp mayonnaise
360g provolone cheese slices

1. Preheat your BBQ over high heat. Oil the steaks with 3 to 4 tsp of the oil and then season liberally with salt & pepper. Toss the prepared onions and peppers with 1 tbsp of the oil.
2. Turn the heat on your BBQ to medium or medium/high and grill the steaks until your desired doneness, approximately 4 to 6 minutes per side for medium (depending on the temperature of the steaks and the power of your BBQ). Grill the onion and pepper slices at the same time just until they are somewhat charred and cooked through. Remove the steaks, onions and peppers and set aside.
3. Melt the butter and garlic together and set aside.
4. Slice the peppers into thin strips and rough chop the onions. Toss these pepper and onion pieces together with the Worcestershire and season to taste with salt & pepper. Set aside.

5. Slice the steaks into very thin strips and toss with the reserved garlic butter and season to taste with salt & pepper. Set aside.

6. Prepare the buns by placing the cut side down on the grill and toasting them. Then spread 1 tbsp of mayonnaise on each the top and bottom toasted halves of the buns.

7. Top each open bun with equal amounts of the reserved steak slices, then equal amounts of the reserved onion/pepper mix, and then equal amounts of cheese slices. Place the open faced sandwiches on a baking sheet and broil in the oven until the cheese is thoroughly melted. Serve immediately.

Makes 6 large sandwiches

South-Western Steak Salad

Originally prepared for Lepp Farm Market www.leppfarmmarket.com
Full colour photo available at www.chefdez.com

Steak
2 tbsp paprika
1 tsp black pepper
1 tsp dried oregano
1 tsp salt
1/2 to 1 tsp cayenne pepper
1-700g beef flank steak
4 tbsp butter, melted
1 garlic clove crushed
1 tsp finely chopped parsley
Dressing
2 large soft avocados
Juice of 1 lime
1 cup sour cream

1/2 cup salsa

2 tsp chilli powder

2 tsp salt

Salad

1 large head Romaine lettuce, cut, washed, & dried

1-398ml can black beans, rinsed & drained

1 medium zucchini, quartered lengthwise & sliced

Kernels from 2 ears of fresh corn

1 large red bell pepper, diced small

1. In a small bowl, combine the paprika, pepper, oregano, salt, and cayenne. Liberally coat the steak with this mixture and let sit in the refrigerator for at least 1 hour. Mix the butter, garlic and parsley and set aside.

2. Preheat BBQ grill on high heat. Cook the flank steak for approximately 5-7 minutes per side, with the lid open, over medium-high heat for medium-rare to medium doneness—depending on the thickness of the steak. When done, let rest for at least 3 to 5 minutes before slicing to help retain the juiciness of the meat.

3. While the steak is cooking, slice, pit and peel the avocados into a bowl large enough to make the dressing in. Mash the avocados with the lime juice as soon as possible to help prevent the avocado from oxidizing (turning brown). Mix in the sour cream, salsa, chilli powder, and salt to make the dressing.

4. Prepare 4 large bowls by equally portioning out the following ingredients in this order: Romaine, beans, zucchini, corn, and bell pepper.

5. Top each salad with an equal amount of dressing. Slice the rested steak thinly across the grain and place an equal amount of steak on each salad. Drizzle the meat with the reserved garlic butter and present to your guests . . . allowing them to admire the display before tossing the salad themselves.

Makes 4 large dinner sized salads

5
Kitchen Gadgets & Appliances

Due to a couple of revelations I have had with my food processor recently, I thought it would be appropriate to focus this column on kitchen gadgets and appliances that I find worthy. I usually opt for the manual alternative to kitchen prep—old-fashioned cutting by hand and elbow grease—but sometimes it is not always the best way.

Recently, my wife wanted to make a dish from her childhood that basically consists of layers of thinly sliced potatoes, carrots, and other vegetables. These ingredients along with seasonings and chunks of sausage are cooked together to create a single pot casserole. When it came time to prepare this dish, the die-hard Chef in me reached for my knife, readying myself for the task at hand. "Why don't we use the slicer attachment on our food processor?" exclaimed my wife. After some convincing, I decided to give it a try and was quite impressed with the uniform slices and ease of preparation. To be honest it was the first time in the 15 years that I owned this food processor that I actually used the slicer attachment.

I have also discovered (with subtle pressuring from my wife) that the regular blade of a food processor can also ease the preparation of finely chopping vegetables, as long as caution is used to prevent from pureeing them into oblivion.

A hand-powered kitchen appliance that I love is my all-in-one apple peeler, corer and slicer. A lip on the edge of ones counter is not necessary as it simply suctions to the surface with amazing strength. A single apple is pressed onto the hand-crank and all of these tasks are completed with a number of circular revolutions—perfect to speed up pie/crumble making. And the best part is that I purchased mine in brand new condition at a second hand store for only five dollars.

For small hand tool gadgets, there are a few that I simply cannot (or more correctly, would rather not) live without.

Olive Pitter—This tool resembles a pair of spring-loaded pliers. It has a circular base to hold an olive on one of the ends, and a prod on the other. When squeezed together, the prod inserts into the olive and pushes the pit through the opposite side. It works great on cherries too.

Garlic Press—I have gone through many poorly made garlic presses in the past, but there is one brand that has never let me down. I highly recommend the Switzerland made "Zyliss" brand. I have literally crushed thousands of cloves with this brand, for the past six years, without fail.

Melon Baller—Great for its intended purpose of creating bite-size balls of melon, but works just as well on cheeses and an assortment of fruits and vegetables. Caramelized balls of potato, for example, makes for an appealing side dish.

Although I do tend to be a bit stubborn when it comes to letting go of my knife skills for a gadget or appliance, the time saved in these circumstances is well worth the loss of Chef's pride.

Dear Chef Dez:

I noticed that many Chefs on TV use a flat grater that lies across a bowl to remove zest from citrus fruits. Is the best way to do this?

Charlotte E.
Surrey, BC

Dear Charlotte:

I actually recommend using a "zester." It is a hand tool that has five little circular blades at the end. When it is dragged across a citrus fruit, it produces beautiful curls of zest while leaving the bitter pith behind. Although flat graters remove the zest in small bits, and thus prevent further chopping, there is no guarantee that one will not grate too far into the bitter white pith. Besides, the curls of zest make great garnish!

Black Bean Soup

"The cut sizes for the bacon and vegetables really doesn't matter too much as the whole soup is pureed with a hand blender anyway"

125g bacon slices, cut into smaller pieces
1 small onion, chopped
1 green bell pepper, chopped
1 large carrot, chopped
1 celery stalk, chopped
2 jalapenos, chopped—seeds & membrane removed for mild
3 to 4 garlic cloves, chopped
Salt & pepper
2-540ml cans of black beans, drained & rinsed
3 to 4 cups chicken stock
1 small bunch fresh cilantro, chopped (reserve some for garnish)
1 medium tomato, chopped
2 tsp ground cumin
1/2 cup premade salsa
Salt & Pepper to taste
1/2 cup sour cream, for garnish

1. Add the bacon pieces to a large heavy bottomed pot over medium high heat and cook until fat has been rendered from the bacon. Cooked but not necessarily crisp, stirring occasionally.
2. Turn the heat down to medium and add the diced onions, green peppers, carrots, celery, jalapenos, garlic, and some salt & pepper to the bacon and bacon fat. Cover and cook until the vegetables are mostly soft, approximately 5 to 7 minutes.
3. Add the black beans and 3 cups of the chicken stock.
4. Add the cilantro, tomatoes, cumin, and salsa. Puree with a hand blender until smooth. Use the remaining 1 cup of chicken stock to thin the soup to your desired consistency while pureeing. Season with salt and pepper to taste.

5. Heat to desired temperature and serve each bowl garnished with a dollop of sour cream and a sprig of cilantro

Makes approximately 10 cups

Hummus in a Pressure Cooker

"Using a pressure cooker you can prepare hummus anytime without soaking the chick peas"

1 cup dry chick peas
4 cups water
3 garlic cloves
1/4 cup tahini or smooth peanut butter
3 tbsp fresh lemon juice
1 tbsp extra virgin olive oil
2-3 tbsp reserved cooking liquid
1 tsp ground cumin
1/2 to 1 tsp salt

1. Add the chick peas and water to the pressure cooker. Close and lock the lid in place and heat to build pressure. Turn down the heat and cook for 50-60 minutes and adjust the heat if necessary to maintain pressure on high pressure (if steam is being released, lower the heat further).
2. Release the pressure following your manufacturer's recommendation. Remove the cooked chick peas from the liquid and let cool. Remember to reserve the residual cooking liquid.
3. While waiting for the chick peas to cool, process the garlic in a food processor until finely minced.
4. To the food processor, add the cooled chick peas, tahini or peanut butter, lemon juice, olive oil, chick pea liquid, cumin, and salt. Process until smooth and serve.

Makes approximately 2 cups

Individual Pineapple Cheesecake Desserts

"Make sure you use canned pineapple as fresh pineapple has a natural enzyme Bromelain that inhibits gelatine from setting. Canned pineapple is cooked in the canning process and thus the enzyme is neutralized. The skim milk powder helps to keep the whipped cream from separating."

2 cans of pineapple tidbits
6 tbsp sugar
1 packet powdered gelatine
250g cream cheese
2 tsp cornstarch dissolved in 1 tbsp reserved pineapple juice
375ml whipping cream
1 & 1/2 tsp skim milk powder
1/2 tsp vanilla essence
1/2 cup nuts, toasted and chopped
Fresh mint leaves, for garnish

1. Place each can of pineapple in separate pots, reserving 1 tbsp of the juice to dissolve the cornstarch. Add 2 tablespoons of sugar to each pot. Turn on low heat. Add gelatine to one of the pots and let dissolve as it heats.
2. Puree the gelatine/pineapple mix with the cream cheese with a hand blender while heating. Set aside by refrigerating until mostly cool.
3. Puree the other pot of pineapple and add the cornstarch/juice mixture. Bring to a boil to thicken. Transfer mixture to a bowl and refrigerate until thoroughly chilled.
4. Whip together the cream, skim milk powder, vanilla, and the last two tablespoons of sugar until firm peaks. Fold the whipped cream with the cooled cream cheese mixture. Spoon into wine glasses or ramekins and chill until firm.
5. Top the individual cheesecake desserts with the pineapple sauce, toasted nuts and sprigs of mint.

Makes eight 1/2 cup portions

Scalloped Potatoes Gratin

Recipe created by Katherine Desormeaux (Mrs. Chef Dez) www.chefdez.com

"These are my favorite scalloped potatoes"

4 large russet potatoes
1 large yellow onion
3 tbsp butter
1 cup grated old cheddar
1 cup milk
2 tbsp flour
2 cups whipping cream
1 clove garlic, finely minced
Salt & pepper

1. Preheat oven to 350 degrees Fahrenheit.
2. Thinly slice potatoes and onion on a mandolin.
3. Butter a casserole dish with 1 tbsp of the butter. Layer the potatoes, onion, and cheddar in 3 layers, seasoning each layer liberally with salt & pepper as you go, ending with cheddar on top.
4. Snake the milk and flour together in a well sealed container. Combine this mixture with the cream and the garlic. Pour over the potatoes and top with the remaining 2 tbsp butter broken into small chunks.
5. Bake for 60 to 75 minutes until potatoes are tender. Let stand for at least 10 minutes before serving.

6

A Meat Thermometer is Worth its Weight in Gold

Over the years I have discovered many simple methods that will help to easily perfect the meals that we serve. Some are so obvious, like a meat thermometer, it is bizarre when I come across a household that does not have one.

Always during the approach of traditional holidays like Thanksgiving, Christmas, and Easter I seem to get bombarded with questions about how long a turkey should cook. Although I appreciate the opportunity for helping people in the kitchen, the answer to me always seems so obvious that it is surprising that more people don't already have the solution. Not only will a simple oven-proof meat thermometer help to save your turkey dinner, it will also be the resolution to mastering the doneness of a myriad of meat roasting recipes. I have owned my current meat thermometer for probably close to fifteen years now and it is still going strong. Not bad for an investment of only a few dollars.

Be certain that you are purchasing one that is heat resistant (oven proof) so that it can be left in the piece of meat for the entire cooking process. If an instant read thermometer is used instead, and the temperature is checked at a number of intervals, valued juices will be lost from the meat with each puncture. One of the most important goals in cooking meat is to keep it moist while still reaching the desired doneness.

The area of a turkey where the thermometer should be inserted is the thickest part of the inner thigh without touching the bone. A stuffed turkey should be done when it reads 180F (82C), and unstuffed at 170F (77C). You should also notice that the legs move easily when twisted and the juices run clear. There is a difference in these two temperature readings because a stuffed turkey is denser, and the stuffing needs to reach a high enough temperature to kill any bacteria present.

This being said, I do realize that people appreciate approximate cooking times to effectively coordinate side dishes to the main course, and it is for this reason only that I will provide guidelines for you. Do not use these parameters as your main indication of doneness, but rather as an additional plan to your trusty meat thermometer. For example, if you cook your turkey in a 325F (160C) oven then allow for this approximation in time:

WEIGHT	UNSTUFFED	STUFFED
3-3.5kg (6.5-8 lbs)	2.5-2.75 hours	3-3.25 hours
3.5-4.5kg (8-10 lbs)	2.75-3 hours	3.25-3.5 hours
4.5-5.5kg (10-12 lbs)	3-3.25 hours	3.5-3.75 hours
5.5-7kg (12-15.5 lbs)	3.25-3.5 hours	3.75-4 hours
7-10kg (15.5-22 lbs)	3.5-4 hours	4-4.5 hours

There are many factors for example that will play havoc on the final accuracy of the cooking time: the temperature of the turkey prior to roasting, the temperature of the stuffing (if used), or maybe your oven is running a bit hotter or colder than the set temperature.

Where you decide to purchase your meat thermometer is not important, as they are available almost everywhere. What is important is that you get one and enjoy the benefits of it for years to come.

Dear Chef Dez:

I heard that it important to let a (turkey) "rest" when it comes out of the oven, before carving it. Is this true, and why?

Brad B.
Abbotsford, BC

Dear Brad:

This is true. Actually it is true with all cuts of meat. The "resting" period gives the meat time to adjust coming from the extreme heat to room temperature. During the cooking process, the high heat causes the atoms in the molecular structure of the meat to move at a high rate of speed. If the meat is cut into soon after it has been removed from the oven, grill, or pan, it will lose a large degree of its vital juices that keep it moist and flavourful.

Boneless Turkey Roast

Originally prepared for Lepp Farm Market www.leppfarmmarket.com
Full colour photo available at www.chefdez.com

"A turkey thigh wrapped up in a turkey breast gives will please all turkey lovers. Wrapping it with bacon not only gives it great flavour, but also helps to protect it from drying out. Serve this with your favourite cranberry sauce."

1 boneless turkey breast, approximately 1kg
Salt & pepper
2 tbsp minced onion
2 tbsp chopped fresh sage
1 garlic clove, minced
1 boneless turkey thigh, approximately 350g
6 to 8 strips of bacon

1. Preheat oven to 325 degrees Fahrenheit.
2. Cut the thickest part of the breast in half (without cutting all the way through) to make the breast more consistent in thickness (butterfly cut) and allow the breast to spread out more (have more surface area).
3. With the skin-side down, season with salt and pepper, and evenly scatter the onion, sage, and garlic over the breast.
4. Remove and discard the skin from the thigh. Lay the thigh on the seasoned breast and then season the thigh with more salt & pepper.
5. Starting with the end of the breast, roll up the thigh inside the breast meat to form a football shape, tucking in the parts of the breast that may be sticking out. Season the top of the breast skin with more salt and pepper.
6. Lay strips of the bacon lengthwise, side by side, on the top of the roast until it is covered. Carefully tie butcher's twine every two inches in the opposite direction of the bacon strips, to secure the roast. Then tie one more piece of butcher's twine lengthwise around the roast (the same direction of the bacon strips).
7. Place the tied roast on a rack in a roasting pan and insert an oven proof thermometer. Roast in the oven for approximately 30 minutes per pound until the

internal temperature reaches 165 degrees Fahrenheit, approximately 1 hour and 45 minutes.

8. Remove from the oven, carefully remove the butcher's twine, and let rest for at least 10 minutes before carving. Serve with your favourite cranberry sauce and enjoy!

Makes 6 to 8 portions

Grilled Bacon Wrapped Meatballs

Originally prepared for Lepp Farm Market www.leppfarmmarket.com
Full colour photo available at www.chefdez.com

"Ground chuck is the perfect meat for meatballs as it is screaming with beefy flavour—combine this with bacon and you couldn't ask for a better dish! Using double pronged skewers will also help with keeping the bacon on the meatballs and for ease of turning the meat while cooking—and also make sure you soak the skewers in water for 24 to 48 hours to prevent them from burning."

2 pounds ground chuck

2 large eggs

1/2 cup fine bread crumbs

1/4 cup finely minced onion

2 tbsp finely minced garlic

2 tsp dried basil

2 tsp dried oregano

2 tsp salt

1 tsp pepper

20 strips of bacon

13 double-pronged skewers, soaked in water for 24 hours minimum, then drained

2 cups strained tomatoes, or tomato sauce

1 cup blueberry jam

1/2 cup brown sugar

1/2 cup white vinegar
2.5 tsp salt
2 tsp Worcestershire sauce

1. In a large bowl, combine the ground chuck, eggs, bread crumbs, onion, garlic, basil, oregano, salt and pepper. Mix thoroughly and then roll into 39 meatballs—they should each be approximately 1 inch in size.
2. Cut the bacon slices in half. Wrap each meatball with a half slice of bacon and skewer immediately to prevent them from becoming unwrapped—place 3 bacon wrapped meatballs in the same direction on each skewer.
3. Preheat your BBQ grill over high heat. Grill the meatball skewers over high heat to sear the outside of the meatballs—approximately 3-4 minutes on each of the 2 sides of the meatballs (don't sear the bacon sides yet as it will cause too many flare ups).
4. Turn off the burner below the skewers (while keeping other burner(s) on), lower the lid of your BBQ and cook with this indirect heat for approximately 25 minutes while maintaining a 325 degree Fahrenheit temperature on the gauge on the lid of your BBQ. When cooked, the internal temperature of the meatballs should read as 71 degrees Celsius on an instant read thermometer.
5. Place the cooked skewers over high heat to sear the 2 bacon sides now until bacon is browned. Serve with the dipping sauce.
6. While the skewers are cooking, combine the strained tomatoes, jam, brown sugar, vinegar, salt, and Worcestershire in a small pot on the side burner and cook until heated thoroughly, stirring frequently. Puree with a hand blender until smooth.

Makes 39 meatballs (3 per skewer)

Prime Rib Roast

Originally prepared for Lepp Farm Market www.leppfarmmarket.com
Full colour photo available at www.chefdez.com

There are a number of tips to cooking a prime rib roast to perfection. The most important is to use a meat thermometer. You can choose from an oven-proof one that is inserted at the beginning of the cooking time and left in, or an instant read one that is used to check the internal temperature at chosen intervals (but not left in the oven). Although both work very well to keep your roast from over cooking, I recommend the oven proof one because you simply leave it in the roast. The result is less punctures to the meat and thus more juice retention.

Rare: 120 to 125 degrees F
Medium Rare: 130 to 135 degrees F
Medium: 140 to 145 degrees F
Medium Well: 150 to 155 degrees F
Well Done: 160 degrees F and above

I have also provided an approximate cooking time chart, but I stress that this is just an informal guideline and not to be used in replace of a meat thermometer. There are many variables that a time chart just cannot encompass: temperature of the meat prior to cooking, exact size/shape of the roast, oven temperature accuracy, etc.

Also, the closer you can bring your roast to room temperature before cooking (without jeopardizing food safety and leaving it out too long) will result in a more uniform doneness. If you put a cold roast in the oven the outer parts of the inside flesh will be overdone in comparison to the center of the meat (where you thermometer is inserted). This time chart is loosely based on this procedure with the result of a 130 degree F medium rare result:

Approx. Weight	Oven Temp	Est. Time
4-5 pounds	450/275 deg F	1.25 to 1.5 hours
7-8.5 pounds	450/275 deg F	1.75 to 2.5 hours
9-10.5 pounds	450/275 deg F	2.5 to 3 hours
11-13.5 pounds	450/275 deg F	3 hours to 3.5 hours

In order to create a flavourful crust, start with a cooking temperature of 450 degrees F for the first 15 minutes of the cooking time. Then reduce the oven temperature to 275 degrees F (without removing the roast from the oven) and continue cooking until your desired internal temperature has been reached. This lower temperature for the reaming majority of the cooking time will help to create a more even cooking of the meat.

Also, it is important to note that prime rib roasts should always be cooked with the bones in tact to create more flavour in the meat. The bones also act as a natural rack for the meat to cook on when placed bone side down in your roasting pan. If desired, you can request that the bones be removed and then tied back on for easy removal before carving. By cooking with the bones on the bottom this leaves the fat cap on the top of the roast for maximum protection from drying out.

If a simple dipping "Au Jus" is desired for serving, remove the roast from the pan and remove almost all of the liquid fat, but leaving the beef drippings in the pan. Put the pan on the burners of your stove. Add 2 parts beef stock and 1 part red wine. Boil until reduced by half in volume. Season with salt & pepper to taste.

Prime Rib Roast
Making note of all instructions above

1 whole Prime Rib Roast
Kosher salt or other coarse salt
Pepper

1. Preheat the oven to 450 degrees F.
2. Thoroughly rub the roast with the salt and lots of black pepper just prior to going in the oven*
3. Roast in the oven (bone side down) for 15 minutes.
4. Reduce the oven temperature to 275 degrees F and continue roasting until the desired internal temperature of the meat is reached.
5. Remove from the oven and let rest for at least 20 to 40 minutes (depending on the size of the roast) to help ensure juices stay in the roast.

6. Remove the bones and carve as desired. Serve with the optional "Au Jus" as described abve.

*Chef Dez note—only salt the roast just prior to putting in the oven. If salt is left on meat for extended periods of time, juices are drawn to the surface of the meat and will inhibit a good searing of the outer crust.

Rubbed & Grilled Beef Tri Tip au Jus

Originally prepared for Lepp Farm Market www.leppfarmmarket.com
Full colour photo available at www.chefdez.com

"Beef Tri Tip is not the same cut as Sirloin Tip. Tri Tip is a specific triangular muscle located in the hip. It is a specific butcher's cut and it is nicely marbled, tender and one of the most flavorful cuts of beef you'll find. The more marbling also makes it juicier and thus the perfect grilling steak. This cut is a butcher's well kept secret to the best tasting beef to come off the grill. . . . and don't forget to buy a thermometer too—you will need one for this recipe!"

2 tbsp sweet smoked paprika
1 tbsp granulated garlic
1 tbsp Mexican chilli powder
2 tsp salt
1 tsp ground black pepper
1 tsp dried oregano leaves
1/2 tsp ground cumin
1 beef Tri Tip, approximately 2 pounds (908g)
1 tbsp canola oil

Au Jus
1 cup full bodied red wine
3 garlic cloves, peeled and cut in half
1 sprig fresh rosemary

1 cup beef broth
1/2 tsp salt
1/2 tsp sugar

1. In a small bowl combine the paprika, granulated garlic, chilli powder, 2 tsp salt, black pepper, oregano, and cumin together.
2. Coat the Tri Tip with the canola oil, then completely coat the Tri Tip with the combined rub from the step above. Let sit for 1 hour to allow the meat to reach more room temperature and let the flavours penetrate the meat.
3. While the meat is sitting, prepare the Jus dipping sauce by combining the red wine, garlic cloves, and rosemary in a small pot. Boil over medium/high to high heat until the wine has reduced in volume by half (one half cup). Add the beef stock, 1/2 tsp salt and 1/2 tsp sugar. Stir to combine, cover and set aside off the heat until the Tri Tip has been cooked.
4. Preheat your BBQ over high heat until very hot. Grill the Tri Tip over medium to medium/high heat (depending on the BTU's of your BBQ) for approximately 8 to 15 minutes per side until the internal temperature of the meat reaches 130 to 135 degrees Fahrenheit for medium rare (check with either an oven proof meat thermometer or an instant read thermometer). Remove from the grill and let sit for at least 10 to 15 minutes before cutting.
5. While the steak is resting, warm the Jus in the pot until hot, drain the garlic and rosemary out and portion into small dipping cups for serving.
6. Carve the Tri Tip against the grain for the maximum tenderness and serve immediately with the Jus dipping cups.

Makes 4 to 6 Portions

Turkey Meatloaf with Cranberry Glaze

Originally prepared for Lepp Farm Market www.leppfarmmarket.com
Full colour photo available at www.chefdez.com

"By using turkey thigh instead of turkey breast, it produces a more moist and flavourful loaf"

Glaze/Topping
1-340g bag of fresh cranberries (or thawed from frozen)
3/4 cup dark brown sugar
1/2 cup ketchup
1/4 tsp salt

Meatloaf
1.5 pounds (681g) ground turkey thigh
1 cup fine bread crumbs
3/4 cup minced onion
3 large eggs
3 garlic cloves, minced
1 tbsp salt
2 tsp ground dry sage
1/2 tsp pepper

1. Preheat the oven to 350 degrees Fahrenheit and prepare a standard size bread loaf pan by lining it with parchment paper (make sure there is enough of the parchment paper sticking out of the pan for easy extraction of the whole loaf when cooked).

2. In a heavy bottomed medium size pot, add all of the ingredients for the Glaze/Topping. Turn heat to medium-high and cook stirring frequently while also mashing with a potato masher as the berries cook and break down, until a smooth thick consistency is reached, approximately 15 minutes.

3. Add all of the meatloaf ingredients to a large bowl and mix thoroughly. Press into the prepared loaf pan and cover with the cranberry topping. Bake for approximately 1 to 1.25 hours until the internal temperature of the meat loaf has reached a minimum of 165 degrees Fahrenheit. Let rest for at least 15 minutes before extracting from the pan. Slice and serve immediately.

Makes 1 loaf

7
Culinary Resolutions

Ah, the start of a fresh year. What better time is there to make a pact with oneself to start anew? In the position of a culinary instructor, I encounter many situations with people wanting to improve areas of the culinary arts within their home kitchens and lifestyles. If you are undecided about making a resolution, contemplate making one focusing on the culinary aspect in your life.

The most common culinary resolution would be one of dietetic boundaries. Many people have the aspiration to start the New Year with a promise of either losing weight or getting in better physical shape. The change in what you consume on a daily basis will obviously influence your success, or lack there of. Try making a resolution to yourself to investigate low fat, low carbohydrate, and/or high protein cooking. This promise will involve educating yourself in these areas, and putting the acquired information into practice. Go to the library, research the Internet, buy a cookbook, and take a cooking class.

Maybe a more suited resolution would be to revamp the state of your pantry and the food supply in your kitchen. Perhaps you have always wanted to have a pantry that is more focused on your favorite cuisines. For example, someone who loves Italian and Greek cuisine would stock their pantry with varying types of olives, capers, tomatoes, grape leaves, olive oils, balsamic vinegars, etc. The refrigerator and freezer can also be coordinated to contain the perishables of the same cuisine. Motivation to focus more on cooking certain cuisines in your household will start with having the ingredients at your fingertips. One can even take this to the extreme in organization by creating labels and segregating areas in your pantry for different food groupings.

The simplest of all culinary resolutions however, would be to blow dust off your cookbooks and start making some new dishes. Whether it is of small or large proportions, we all have collections of cookbooks . . . with many of them going unused. Make it a goal in your home to open up a cookbook once or twice a week, and try a new recipe. If you choose to do this, make sure you are setting yourself up for success. Decide on and investigate the recipe prior to the date you plan on making it. Purchase the ingredients ahead of time, and ensure that you have the basic equipment and utensils necessary to successfully complete the task at hand. This will help eliminate any stress that you may encounter during preparation.

"Attitude is everything". This is the best advice I can give you. Whatever you approach in life, from making a resolution, making new friends or making a new recipe, proceed in a positive fashion. You will always find what you are searching for. If you look for the positives in something or someone, you will always find them. The same applies if you are seeking out negatives. Be aware of what you are looking for and your experience will always be more rewarding.

Dear Chef Dez:
   I noticed in your "Healthy Choices" class, you mention that you had a significant weight loss years ago within a 6-month period. How did you do it?

Tony R.
Abbotsford, BC

Dear Tony:
   I did this by exercising and limiting fat grams—I didn't count calories. The more lean muscle mass a body has, the more calories the body will burn—even when sleeping. Therefore, going to the gym is extremely important. Calories are energy and too many times prior I wasted my efforts limiting them too extensively in my total food intake. Without enough calories in my diet, I never had enough energy to maintain a regular exercise program.
   Please keep in mind that I am not a dietician or medical professional. Everybody is different and I believe that a successful method exists for everyone.

Broiled Italian Tomatoes

12 medium Roma tomatoes, room temperature
Salt & freshly cracked pepper
1/3 cup finely chopped fresh basil
Extra virgin olive oil
150g-200g grated parmiggiano reggiano

1. Slice the tomatoes lengthwise (from core to bottom) into halves. Place the 24 halves, cut side up on a baking sheet (line with parchment for easy clean up).
2. Season liberally with salt and fresh cracked pepper.
3. Distribute the amount of chopped basil evenly on the tomatoes.
4. Drizzle a small amount of olive oil on each tomato.
5. Distribute the cheese evenly on the tomatoes. *Tip—hold each tomato half over the cheese bowl to catch any cheese that falls off, and then return them to the baking sheet.
6. Broil under a hot preheated broiler for approximately 4 to 5 minutes until the cheese is just starting to brown.

Makes 24 halves

Carrot Bran Muffins

1 & 1/2 cups whole wheat flour
1 & 1/2 cups natural bran
1/3 cup SPLENDA® Brown Sugar Blend
1/4 cup ground flax seed
2 tsp baking soda
1 & 1/2 tsp ground cinnamon
1/2 tsp salt
1/4 tsp ground cloves
1/4 tsp ground nutmeg
1 cup finely grated carrot
2 large eggs
1 & 1/2 cups milk
1/4 cup unsweetened apple sauce
1/4 cup canola oil
2 tbsp lemon juice

1. Preheat oven to 400° F (200 °C) and prepare a 12 cup muffin pan with baking spray.
2. Combine the whole wheat flour, natural bran, SPLENDA® Brown Sugar Blend, ground flax seed, baking soda, ground cinnamon, salt, ground cloves, and ground nutmeg in a mixing bowl.
3. Toss the grated carrot into this dry mixture.
4. Beat the eggs thoroughly in a separate bowl.
5. Add the milk, apple sauce, canola oil, and lemon juice to the beaten eggs. Continue beating until thoroughly combined.
6. Combine the mixtures in the two bowls together until just mixed. Do not over mix.
7. Spoon the batter equally into the prepared muffin pan.
8. Bake for 20 minutes.
9. Cool slightly in the pan before serving.

Makes 12 large muffins

Fresh Cut Salsa

"By rinsing and draining the diced red onion, the onion flavour won't be overpowering, but will still provide nice colour. Omit the seeds and white membrane from the jalapeno for a milder salsa."

3 large Roma tomatoes, diced small
1 small yellow bell pepper, diced small
1/2 long English cucumber, diced small
1 cup small diced red onion, rinsed and drained
1 jalapeno, diced very small
1-2 garlic cloves, crushed
Juice of 1 lime
1 tsp sugar
Salt & Pepper to taste
Fresh chopped cilantro, to taste

- Mix everything together and enjoy!

Makes approximately 4 cups

Holiday Cranberry Buttermilk Scones

"Whether for breakfast or with an afternoon coffee, these scones filled with cranberries and warm spices offer up an unforgettable treat"

1 cup whole wheat flour
1 cup all purpose flour
1/2 cup SPLENDA® No Calorie Sweetener, Granulated
2 tsp baking powder
2 tsp baking soda
1 & 1/2 tsp ground cinnamon

1/2 tsp salt

1/4 tsp ground cloves

1/4 tsp ground nutmeg

1/2 cup butter, cold or frozen

1/2 cup frozen cranberries, halved or coarsely chopped

1 cup buttermilk

1 & 1/2 tbsp buttermilk

2 tbsp SPLENDA® No Calorie Sweetener, Granulated

1/2 tsp ground cinnamon

1. Preheat oven to 425° F (220 °C) and prepare a baking sheet with baking spray or line it with parchment paper.
2. Combine the whole wheat flour, all purpose flour, the 1/2 cup SPLENDA® Granulated, baking powder, the 1 & 1/2 teaspoons cinnamon, salt, cloves, and nutmeg together in a mixing bowl.
3. Grate the butter into the dry mixture with a coarse size grater. Stop at intervals to lightly toss the butter particles into the flour mixture to keep the butter from lumping together.
4. Add the cranberries and toss into this mixture.
5. Mix in the 1 cup of buttermilk until the dough is just starting to combine. Turn out onto countertop and knead until the dough just comes together and forms a smooth ball. DO NOT OVERMIX. Lightly flour the surface of the dough and gently press into a flat round disc approximately 3/4 inch (2cm) thick. Transfer the dough to the prepared baking sheet.
6. Brush the 1 & 1/2 tablespoons of buttermilk over the surface of the dough.
7. Mix the 2 tablespoons of SPLENDA® Granulated with the one half teaspoon of cinnamon and evenly sprinkle this mix over the surface of the dough.
8. Cut the dough into 8 equal pie shaped sections, but do not separate them—keep the disc in one large circle. This will help support the sides of each portion as they rise in the oven.
9. Bake for 20 minutes until golden brown.
10. Cut the sections to separate and serve immediately with butter, if desired.

Makes 8 scones

Mediterranean Olive Tofu Crostini

Full colour photo available at www.chefdez.com

"Crostini is Italian for fried bread and is traditionally served with a topping. I have combined crumbled medium firm tofu with kalamata olives and a handful of other Mediterranean ingredients and marinated them together. Topped on olive oil broiled Italian bread makes this a wonderful appetizer or brunch item."

1 cup kalamata olives, pitted and chopped

115g medium firm tofu, drained and crumbled

2 tsp anchovy paste

1 garlic clove, crushed to a paste

1 tbsp chopped fresh oregano

1 tbsp chopped fresh basil

1/4 tsp fresh cracked pepper

1 tbsp extra virgin olive oil

2 tsp fresh lemon juice

1/2 tsp sugar

3 slices from a round crusty bread loaf, cut in half

1 to 2 tbsp extra virgin olive oil

1. Mix the olives, tofu, anchovy, garlic, oregano, basil, pepper, 1 tbsp oil, lemon juice, and sugar in a bowl. Cover and let sit for a few hours or refrigerate overnight. If refrigerated, bring to room temperature before assembling/serving.
2. Brush the 1 to 2 tbsp of extra virgin olive oil on the bread slices and broil for 2 to 3 minutes until toasted.
3. Top the toasted bread slices with equal amounts of the tofu mixture and serve immediately.

Makes 6 portions

Pineapple Muesli Yogurt Parfaits

Full colour photo available at www.chefdez.com

"If you do not want to use Splenda, replace it with a sugar that dissolve and blend easily with the yogurt, such as maple syrup, agave syrup, or a few drops of stevia . . . or leave out the added sweetness altogether."

Muesli Ingredients

2/3 cup large flake oats
1/3 cup bran flakes cereal
1/3 cup slivered almonds
1/3 cup sweetened coconut
3 tbsp wheat germ
1 tbsp sesame seeds
1 tbsp ground flax seed
1/2 tsp ground cinnamon
1/4 tsp salt
3 tbsp canola oil
1 & 1/2 tbsp liquid honey

Yogurt Ingredients

2-398ml cans crushed pineapple
1-750g container plain low fat yogurt
6 tbsp SPLENDA® No Calorie Sweetener, Granulated
1/2 tsp vanilla extract

1. Preheat oven to 400° F (200 °C).
2. Combine and mix all of the dry Muesli ingredients in a mixing bowl. Whisk the canola oil and liquid honey together and drizzle over the combined dry mixture. Stir well to combine thoroughly and distribute this mixture evenly onto a baking sheet.
3. Bake for approximately 15 minutes, stirring every 5 minutes to ensure the mixture does not burn. Remove from the oven and cool at room temperature on the baking sheet—the mixture will crisp as it cools on the baking sheet.

4. Strain the canned crushed pineapple in a wire strainer. Transfer the strained pineapple to a clean linen towel, or cheesecloth, and squeeze to remove the excess liquid.

5. Combine the strained pineapple with the yogurt, Splenda, and vanilla in a mixing bowl.

6. Assemble the parfaits in four 300ml parfait glasses or four 300ml brandy snifters as follows: in each glass place one half cup yogurt mixture, then one quarter cup muesli, then another one half cup yogurt mixture, and top with a final one quarter cup muesli mixture.

7. Serve immediately. The muesli & yogurt mixtures can be made ahead of time, but do not assemble them together until just before serving to prevent the muesli mixture from going soggy.

Makes 4 portions

Vinegar Coleslaw Dressing

Recipe created by Katherine Desormeaux (Mrs. Chef Dez) www.chefdez.com

"A great alternative to high fat mayonnaise based coleslaw dressings. Mix with 5 cups of shredded cabbage or coleslaw mix."

1/4 cup white sugar
1/4 cup white vinegar
2 tbsp canola oil
2 tbsp grated onion
1 tsp yellow or Dijon mustard
1/2 tsp salt
1/2 tsp celery salt
1/4 tsp pepper

1. Mix together thoroughly and toss with 5 cups shredded cabbage or coleslaw mix.

8

"Oven Dried" Tomatoes instead of "Sun Dried"

If you like tomatoes, chances are you also love the taste of robust sun-dried tomatoes. They can be purchased either packed in oil, vacuum packed, or dehydrated; and when buying them from the store, I like the ones packed in oil the best. The ones made from scratch however, are even tastier.

Whatever the process, dried tomatoes are more concentrated in flavor because most of the water content has been removed during the drying process. Although this recipe is called Oven "Dried" Tomatoes, they are not really dried; they are still moist but have just shrunk to approximately one-third to one-quarter of their original size and have really intense flavour. We love using these in a number of recipes such as pasta, pizza, sandwiches, or even just eating them on their own in an Italian antipasto platter with a number of other bite sized tidbits. The downside of this recipe is the length of time they need to be in the oven. Cooking them at a low temperature for a long period of time is the best way to extract moisture, intensify flavours, without burning them in the process. Close attention is needed in the latter part of the cooking process to ensure that they do not get overcooked, dried out, and/or burnt. The cooking time is an approximation and will depend on a number of factors: the size of the tomatoes, the ripeness of the tomatoes, the correct calibration of your oven, etc. Do not let this scare you however, just pay attention, that's all.

This is a great recipe to make on a day when you are going to be home anyway and want the warm Mediterranean aromas filling your house. Since they are not completely dried however, they do not last indefinitely. Once cooled, store them in an airtight container and keep refrigerated for up to 7 days. Enjoy!

Oven Dried Tomatoes

"If you can spare the time, the roasting of the tomatoes in the oven is well worth it—they become so intense in flavour! Make extra tomatoes and add them to pasta, sandwiches, salads, etc."

10 Roma tomatoes
2 tbsp olive oil
2 tbsp balsamic vinegar
1 tbsp dried basil leaves (not ground)
1 tbsp dried oregano leaves (not ground)
1/2 tsp salt
1/2 tsp fresh cracked pepper

1. Preheat oven to 200 degrees Fahrenheit.
2. Remove and discard any green tops of the tomatoes, slice in half from top to bottom (lengthwise), and place them in a mixing bowl.
3. Add the olive oil, balsamic vinegar, basil, oregano, salt, pepper, and toss to coat. Gently work a small amount of pulp out of tomato halves while working the flavourings into the tomato cavities.
4. Arrange the tomatoes cut side up on a baking sheet lined with parchment paper.
5. Spoon the remaining liquid from the bowl over the tomatoes and lightly season each one again with salt and pepper.

6. Bake for approximately 5 to 6 hours, until the tomatoes have reduced by approximately two-thirds or three-quarters in size but are still moist. Remove from the oven and cool to room temperature.

7. Use in a number of recipes such as pastas, pizzas, bruscetta, grains, etc ... anywhere you want incredible tomato flavor.

Makes 20 halves

Mediterranean Pasta with Grilled Chicken

"A rosé pasta dish made with both fresh & sun-dried tomatoes. Finished with brandy, fresh basil, and topped with grilled chicken."

4 boneless skinless chicken breasts
1 tbsp canola oil
Salt & pepper
300g dry linguine
2 tbsp olive oil
1 large tomato, sliced into thin julienne strips
1/2 cup oil packed sun-dried tomatoes, drained and sliced thin
1/2 cup thinly sliced red onion
2 tbsp canned soft green peppercorns
8 cloves garlic, finely minced, or crushed into a paste
2 tbsp lemon juice
1 tbsp sugar
2 tsp salt
1/2 tsp pepper
1 cup whipping cream
1/4 cup brandy
1/4 cup chopped fresh basil

1. Butterfly the chicken breasts to make them thinner and more even thickness. Coat with the canola oil and season with salt & pepper. Grill on your BBQ until done, approximately 3 to 5 minutes per side over medium-high to high heat.
2. Boil the pasta to desired doneness.
3. In a bowl combine the olive oil, tomato, sun-dried tomato, onion, peppercorns, garlic, lemon juice, sugar, salt, and pepper.
4. When the pasta and the chicken are approximately half done, heat a large pan over medium high heat. When hot add the bowl of ingredients from step 3 and cook while stirring occasionally for approximately 2 to 3 minutes.
5. Stir in the cream and bring to a boil. At the moment when it just reaches a boil, carefully add the brandy and carefully ignite with a long lighter or match. Shake the pan lightly until the flames subside and sauce thickens slightly.
6. Toss in the pasta and the fresh basil. Plate the four portions and top with a grilled chicken breast on each.

Makes 4 portions

Sausage, Tomato & Herb Frittata

Originally prepared for Lepp Farm Market www.leppfarmmarket.com
Full colour photo available at www.chefdez.com
"Using sundried tomatoes, instead of fresh tomatoes, offer more robust flavour. Also use true Italian Parmigiano Reggiano as your parmesan cheese of choice."

2 tbsp extra virgin olive oil
500g mild Italian sausages, removed from casings
1 medium onion, diced small
6 garlic cloves, minced
1 cup oil packed sundried tomatoes, drained and finely chopped
1/4 cup finely chopped fresh basil
1/4 cup finely chopped fresh oregano

2 tsp salt
1/2 tsp pepper
12 large eggs
1.25 cups grated Parmigiano Reggiano
Sour cream, optional

1. Preheat the oven to 350 degrees Fahrenheit and prepare a 10-inch round baking dish by spraying it with baking spray.
2. Add olive oil, sausage meat, onion and garlic to a frying pan and cook over medium heat for approximately 10 to 15 minutes until the sausage meat is cooked and the onion and garlic are soft. Stir occasionally breaking up the sausage meat into small bits as it cooks.
3. Transfer cooked sausage mixture to a large mixing bowl. Add the sundried tomatoes, basil, oregano, salt, pepper, eggs, and ¾ (three quarters) cup of the grated parmesan cheese. Combine thoroughly together.
4. Pour the mixture into the prepared pan and take care to spread evenly. Top evenly with the remaining ½ (one half) cup of parmesan cheese. Bake for approximately 60 minutes until firm and lightly browned. The center of the frittata should not jiggle.
5. Remove from the oven and let stand on a cooling rack for at least 15 minutes before cutting and serving. Optional: serve with dollops of sour cream.

Makes 8-12 Portions

Sundried Tomato Butter Sauce

Full colour photo available at www.chefdez.com

"This sauce is extremely thick like a 'topping' rather than a 'sauce,' but I like it that way. If you want it saucier either whisk in more butter, or reduce the amount of sundried tomatoes. The whisking of air into the butter is important to create a sauce consistency—without doing this you will end up with just a greasy mess of melted butter."

2 tbsp minced onion

3 to 4 garlic cloves

6 tbsp white wine

3 tbsp white wine vinegar

1 cup chopped oil packed sundried tomatoes, drained

4 tbsp whipping cream

1 tsp sugar

1/4 tsp salt

1/4 tsp pepper

3/4 cup cold butter, cut in small pieces

1. Add onion, garlic, wine, and vinegar to a saucepan. Bring to a boil over medium-high to high heat, and reduce until there is only 1 to 2 tablespoons of liquid left in the pan.

2. Add the sundried tomatoes and stir to heat. Stir in the whipping cream, sugar, salt and pepper and heat just slightly, approximately 5 to 10 seconds.

3. Remove from the heat and whisk in the butter one piece at a time until it forms a sauce.

4. Serve immediately on fish or chicken.

Makes approximately 1.25 cups

Sun Dried Tomato Hummus

3 garlic cloves
1-540ml can of chickpeas, drained, reserving liquid
1/2 cup oil packed sundried tomatoes, drained, reserving oil
1/4 cup smooth peanut butter
3 tbsp fresh lemon juice
1 tbsp oil reserved from the sundried tomatoes
2-3 tbsp chickpea liquid
1 tsp cumin
1/2 to 1 tsp salt

1. Place garlic cloves in food processor and mince.
2. Add all other ingredients and process until smooth.
3. Serve with pita bread

Makes approximately 1.5 cups.

9

Pumpkins are not just for Jack-O-Lanterns

Don't you just love the autumn harvest? The feeling of a crisp breeze in the air, the sound and sight of rustling leaves in a rainbow of colours, and a plentiful array of gourds, squash, and pumpkins available at the produce counter!

Pumpkins are obviously one of the more popular harvests this time of the year. Walking through suburban neighborhoods on Halloween night and gazing at all the eerily lit creations sitting in windows and on front porches can make one hungry—well at least for me! I feel that pumpkin as a food is quite neglected in our everyday diets. Although this bright orange squash is approximately ninety percent water, it is loaded with beta-carotene (an important antioxidant) and a list of nutritional elements that play an important role in a well balanced diet.

Pumpkin is a member of the squash family and, as with all squash, is a fruit. Any product of a plant containing seeds is botanically classified as fruit, just like melons for example. Squashes are closely related to the melon family of plants. There are two main general types of squash—summer squash and winter squash. Summer squash are ones that are not able to be stored for long periods of time. Zucchini would be an excellent representation of a popular summer squash. Winter squash on the other hand can be stored for long periods of time under ideal storage conditions. They should be kept away from light and in an area that is moderately cooler than room temperature. Good ventilation is also necessary. Along with pumpkins, other winter squash are acorn, butternut, and autumn squash.

Pumpkins are most popularly used as jack-o-lanterns on Halloween night, and in varying recipes of pies, cakes, and soups. Rarely does one see pumpkin served at the table on its own. It can be used in any application that one would use other winter squashes, and undeniably will offer more flavour to the dish. Cubes of oven-roasted pumpkin, in a medley of other colourful vegetables, are a perfect accompaniment to an autumn meal. Alternatively, try using small chunks of pumpkin in your next stir-fry or pasta dish. To make preparation easier, cut the pumpkin into workable pieces to aid in peeling and chopping. Winter squashes should always be peeled before consuming. Their tougher skin is often challenging for the traditional vegetable peeler, and therefore a knife may be more facilitating for this task. Afterwards, chop the pumpkin into pieces best suited for the recipe being planned.

As well as the flesh, the seeds are also edible. The seeds are sometimes easily forgotten about, and discarded along with the innards. Roasted pumpkin seeds can easily be prepared, and transforms them into a nutritional snack. Separate the seeds from the extracted inner filaments and lightly coat the seeds with vegetable or olive oil. Toss with salt & pepper, or seasoning salt, if desired, and roast them on a baking sheet in a 450-degree oven, stirring occasionally, until golden brown and crispy, approximately 12 to 15 minutes. Be careful to watch them closely as they burn quite easily. Serve them in a bowl on their own, or with a mixture of other seeds, nuts, and dried fruit. Pumpkin seeds are credited with a number of medicinal properties, and are a great source of numerous minerals. However, due to their high fat content, they should always be consumed in moderation. A serving size of nuts or seeds is equivalent to approximately the size of a golf ball.

Dear Chef Dez:

We always buy cans of pureed pumpkin this time of year for different dessert recipes. Since pumpkins are available fresh, wouldn't it be more economical to make it myself? How do I go about doing this?

John G.
Chilliwack, BC

Dear John:

It can be done quite easily. Cut a fresh pumpkin in half and remove the seeds and the stringy filaments. Place the cut sides down on a baking sheet and bake in a 350-degree oven until the flesh is very tender—approximately one hour. Spoon the cooked flesh off the skin and into a food processor and puree until smooth. Transfer it to a large, fine wire mesh strainer set over a bowl, cover and let drain in the refrigerator overnight. Discard the liquid, and use the drained puree in any fashion that you would with canned.

CHEF DEZ

Healthy Pumpkin Cupcakes

1 & 1/2 cups whole wheat flour
1/2 cup SPLENDA° No Calorie Sweetener, Granulated
1 tsp baking powder
1 tsp baking soda
1 tsp ground cinnamon
1/2 tsp salt
1/2 tsp ground nutmeg
1/4 tsp ground cloves
1 large egg
1 & 3/4 cups canned pumpkin
1/2 cup canola oil

<u>Icing Ingredients</u>
1-250g package spreadable low fat cream cheese
1/2 cup SPLENDA° No Calorie Sweetener, Granulated
1 tsp vanilla extract

1. Preheat oven to 400° F (200 °C) and prepare a 12 cup muffin pan with baking spray.
2. Combine the whole wheat flour, SPLENDA° No Calorie Sweetener Granulated, baking powder, baking soda, ground cinnamon, salt, ground nutmeg, and ground cloves in a mixing bowl.
3. Beat the egg thoroughly in a separate bowl.
4. Add the canned pumpkin and canola oil to the beaten egg. Mix until thoroughly combined.
5. Combine the mixtures in the two bowls together until just mixed. Do not over mix. The batter will be a bit stiffer than a typical cake or muffin batter.
6. Spoon the batter equally into the prepared muffin pan, taking the time to evenly smooth the batter in each cup.
7. Bake for approximately 18 to 20 minutes.
8. Remove from the pan and cool completely on a wire rack.

9. Combine the cream cheese, SPLENDA° No Calorie Sweetener Granulated, and vanilla to form an icing.
10. Spread the icing equally over the tops of the thoroughly cooled cupcakes.

Makes 12 cupcakes

Pumpkin Puree from Scratch (not from a can)

"Since pumpkins are very inexpensive, this is very economical"

1 fresh whole pumpkin

1. Preheat oven to 350 degrees.
2. Cut the pumpkin in half and remove the seeds and scrape out the stringy pulp.
3. Place the cut sides down on a baking sheet and bake until the flesh is very tender, approximately 1 hour.
4. Let cool until safe enough to handle. Spoon the cooked flesh off the skin and into a food processor, in batches. Puree each batch until smooth, scraping down the sides as necessary.
5. Transfer the puree to a large fine wire mesh strainer set over a bowl, cover and let drain in the refrigerator overnight. Discard the liquid, and use the drained puree in any fashion that you would with canned.

Pumpkin Vinaigrette

"Great on greens with roasted pumpkin seeds and dried cranberries"

3/4 cup pumpkin puree
1/4 cup apple cider vinegar
2 tbsp maple syrup
1 tbsp molasses
1 tbsp Dijon or grainy mustard
3/4 tsp salt
1/2 tsp dried thyme leaves
1/4 tsp ground cinnamon
1/4 tsp ground nutmeg
1/4 tsp pepper
3/4 cup extra virgin olive oil

1. Mix all the ingredients, except for the oil, together in a bowl or food processor.
2. While continually mixing (or processing) slowly add the olive oil in a thin stream until completely blended.

Makes approximately 2 cups

Pumpkin Wedge Dessert

"Easier than pumpkin pie for dessert, and uniquely different"

1.2kg of raw pumpkin
1/4 cup brandy
1/4 cup apple juice
1/4 cup dark brown sugar
1/2 tsp ground cinnamon

1/8 tsp ground ginger

1/8 tsp ground cloves

1/8 tsp ground allspice

1/8 tsp ground nutmeg

1/8 tsp salt

1-250g package cream cheese, room temperature

1/2 cup dark corn syrup

1 tsp vanilla extract

Zest of 2 lemons, finely grated or chopped

1. Preheat oven to 350 degrees.
2. Remove the seeds and the stringy pulp from the inside of the pumpkin. Cut the pumpkin into 8 to 12 equal wedges or chunks. Make cuts in the flesh of the pumpkin every half inch without cutting through the skin, and then every half inch in the opposite direction to make a "cross-hatch" design in the flesh while keeping the chunks intact.
3. Mix the brown sugar, cinnamon, ginger, cloves, allspice, nutmeg, and salt together. Spoon/spread this mixture evenly over the flesh of the pumpkin pieces.
4. Pour the brandy and apple juice in a covered oven-safe dish big enough to accommodate the pumpkin pieces in a single layer. Add the pumpkin pieces skin side down. Cover and bake for approximately 70 minutes until tender.
5. While the pumpkin is baking, beat the room temperature cream cheese until smooth and then add the corn syrup, vanilla and zest. Mix well and set aside.
6. Remove the baked pumpkin pieces and plate them individually. Pour the residual liquid from the baking dish into a small sauce pan and reduce by half to three quarters over high heat until syrupy.
7. Distribute an equal amount of the cream cheese mixture on each pumpkin piece. Drizzle with the liquid reduction and serve immediately.

Makes 8 to 12 portions

Roasted Pumpkin Seeds

"Due to their high fat content, they should always be consumed in moderation. A serving size of nuts or seeds is equivalent to approximately the size of a golf ball."

1.5 cups raw pumpkin seeds, rinsed and patted dry
2 tbsp olive oil
2-2.5 tsp seasoning salt

1. Preheat oven to 450 degrees.
2. Toss the seeds with the olive oil and seasoning salt and scatter them on a baking sheet large enough so that they are a single layer.
3. Bake for approximately 8 to 12 minutes until golden brown, tossing them around at 5 minutes and then every two minutes afterwards.
4. Let cool on the baking sheet to crisp up further. Serve them at room temperature.

10

Is Regular Table Salt Acceptable for Cooking?

In today's wonderful world of cuisine, salt has evolved from being just another staple in our pantries to a myriad of choices with considerations based on texture, flavour, and health aspects. From sea salt to exotic salt such as "fleur de sel" or Himalayan pink salt, salt is playing a much larger role in our culinary choices.

With health considerations always affecting more of our daily lives than ever before, regular table salt has taken quite a beating over the past years. More and more recipes are now quoting salts such as "sea" or "kosher" instead of the simple ingredient listing "salt". This is happening because of the larger crystallized shapes and slight flavour attributes that they offer over table salt. Another reason however, is because sea or kosher salts do not have the additives that regular table salt has and thus offer an arguably cleaner taste.

This being said, let's first understand that all salt is the mineral sodium chloride. That's what makes salt, salt. Looking at the ingredient list on a box of table salt from my pantry, it lists the following: salt, calcium silicate, potassium iodide, and sodium thiosulphate. In other words, there are three additives being combined with pure sodium chloride to make the final product: table salt.

Should we avoid table salt because of these additives? In a document I received from the Sifto Salt Corporation, it states that in a statistical study based on production averages in the year 2007, the following ingredient percentages are applicable: Salt (sodium chloride) 99.694%, Calcium Silicate 0.250%, Sodium Thiosulphate 0.048%, and Potassium Iodide at 0.008%. If it is true, that the additives are equal to less than one third of a percent, why are they even there and should we be concerned?

Calcium silicate is added as an anti-caking ingredient to keep the salt free-flowing instead of clumping into a mass. Potassium iodide is what makes table salt iodized and is a source of stable iodine; an important chemical needed by the body to make thyroid hormones and is added to salt to help protect against Iodine Deficiency Disorders. Sodium thiosulphate, from what I can find out, is added in very small quantities to help prevent the oxidization of the iodine.

Everyone has opinions, just like they do taste buds, and my preference is to use and recommend good old table salt when it comes to cooking where the salt is going to be dissolved in moisture with a number of other flavourings and ingredients. Raw applications however, or finishing procedures, would definitely benefit from gourmet salts such as varieties of sea salts and kosher salt. These applications would include raw vegetables, salads and any recipe which requires a finishing salt to be sprinkled on the finished dish. This allows for the consumer of the meal to taste and feel the differences that these gourmet salts have to offer.

To conclude, my advice is to help you save money and make sure you have enough iodine in your diet. Use table salt for everyday cooking except when a finishing salt is needed. When gourmet salts are being dissolved in cooking procedures their characteristics that you are paying for tend to be nonexistent and table salt is a fraction of the price.

Dear Chef Dez:

I see many chefs quoting kosher salt as an ingredient. What is kosher salt and how is it different?

Wayne F.
Fort Frances, ON

Dear Wayne:

Kosher salt is crystallized salt that has no additives and is traditionally used in the koshering process of purifying meats. The salt itself is not kosher per say, but the meat that is cured from this process is labeled "kosher". The crystals of this salt need to be a certain size to efficiently and effectively draw moisture (blood) from meat in order to classify it as "kosher" in the Jewish religion. Chefs will admit that when taking a pinch of kosher salt it is easier to feel how much salt they are adding to a recipe, due to the size of the crystals. I believe that one should let their taste buds be the guide instead . . . but, like taste buds, everyone has an opinion.

Apricot Pecan Pork Chops

Originally prepared for Lepp Farm Market www.leppfarmmarket.com
Full colour photo available at www.chefdez.com

4 cups cold water
1/4 cup salt
1/4 cup brown sugar (not golden sugar)
4-one inch thick bone-in pork chops
100g pecan halves, approximately 3/4 cup
1 tbsp grape seed oil or canola oil
Pepper
1/2 cup white wine
6 garlic cloves, minced
250g dried apricots (approximately 1.75 cups), cut into quarters
1 & 1/2 cups chicken broth
1 tbsp brown sugar (not golden sugar)
1 to 2 tsp sambal oelek
1 tbsp apple cider vinegar
1/4 cup whipping cream

1. Add the water, salt and the quarter cup brown sugar to a large bowl and whisk vigorously until the salt and sugar have dissolved. Place the pork chops in a large freezer bag and pour this brine over them. Squeeze out as much air as possible when closing the bag and then place the bag of brine/chops back into the bowl and refrigerate for 1 to 2 hours.
2. While the chops are brining, toast the pecans and set aside. The pecans can be easily toasted in a small dry pan over medium heat, while tossing occasionally, for approximately 5 to 10 minutes. Watch them carefully as they can burn easily due to their high fat content.
3. Preheat the oven to 425 degrees Fahrenheit. Remove the chops from the brine and pat them dry to remove any excess moisture. Preheat a large heavy bottomed pan over medium-high heat. Coat the chops with the oil and season them with pepper.

4. Once the pan is hot, sear the chops on both sides for approximately 3 to 4 minutes per side. Then transfer the chops to a broiler pan and bake in the oven for approximately 8 to 10 minutes. Remove and let them rest for at least 5 minutes.

5. When the chops are put into the oven, drain any excess fat off the pan. Turn down the stove to medium heat and place the pan back on the heat—immediately add the white wine carefully to the pan to deglaze (scrape the browned bits off the bottom with a wooden spoon). Add the garlic, apricots, chicken broth, 1 tbsp brown sugar, and sambal oelek. Stir to combine and cook for approximately 8 to 10 minutes, stirring occasionally, until it has become syrupy.

6. Stir in the vinegar and whipping cream, and reduce again until syrupy, approximately 2 to 3 minutes more. Serve over the resting chops and garnish with the reserved toasted pecans.

Makes 4 portions

Brined & Grilled Pork Chops with Apple Slaw

Originally prepared for Lepp Farm Market www.leppfarmmarket.com
Full colour photo available at www.chefdez.com

"A wonderful twist on the classic pairing of pork and apples. Using bone-in pork chops will yield not only more flavour but more moisture as well."

1/4 cup table salt**
4 cups cold water
6 bone-in pork chops
1 to 2 tbsp canola oil
Salt & pepper

Apple Slaw
4 cups grated Gala apple (approx. 3 to 4 cored apples)

3 tbsp apple cider vinegar
2 cups shredded purple cabbage
2 cups shredded green cabbage
1/2 cup grated carrot
1 cup mayonnaise, or light mayonnaise
1/2 cup sour cream, or light sour cream
3 tbsp liquid honey
2 tbsp grainy mustard
1 & 1/2 tsp seasoning salt
Freshly cracked pepper to taste

1. In a large bowl, dissolve the salt in the water by whisking vigorously. Submerse the pork chops in this brine. Cover and refrigerate for 1 hour.
2. While the pork is brining, prepare the slaw by putting the grated apple in a large bowl and tossing with the vinegar to help prevent oxidization (going brown). Add the purple cabbage, green cabbage, carrot, mayonnaise, sour cream, honey, mustard, seasoning salt, and pepper. Toss to mix thoroughly and keep refrigerated.
3. When the pork has finished brining, remove the chops from the brine and pat them dry with paper towel. Preheat your BBQ over high heat until hot. Coat the chops with canola oil and seasoned them lightly with salt and pepper (remember that they will already be seasoned with salt from the brine).
4. When your BBQ is hot, place the chops on the grill and turn the heat down to medium-high. Grill the chops for approximately 5 to 8 minutes per side until just cooked—touching them should feel somewhat firm, but not too firm (overcooked).
5. Serve the chops topped with the apple slaw, or on the side, but this recipe shines when both are eaten together in the same bite.

Chef Dez note on this recipe—I have quoted 'table salt' for use in the brine—you can use other salts (kosher, sea, etc) as long as they are the same granule size of table salt. A salt with larger granule size actually has less salt per measure because there are more air pockets around the granules.

Also, this is a basic brine (salt & water)—feel free to add other ingredients to your brine such as sugar, peppercorns, bay leaves, etc.—anything that will infuse flavour into the meat. Brines are the best way to keep meats moist and flavourful during the cooking process—especially lean meats like pork loin and chicken breast.

Makes 6 portions

Pasta Fresca d'Estate

Originally prepared for Lepp Farm Market www.leppfarmmarket.com
Full colour photo available at www.chefdez.com

"Italian for Fresh Summer Pasta. By using a pre-cooked deli chicken, dinner just got a whole lot easier!"

500g pasta: spirali, penne, fussili, etc.
Salt
1/3 cup butter
6 to 8 garlic cloves, minced
1 medium green zucchini, quartered lengthwise & sliced
4 Roma tomatoes, quartered lengthwise & sliced into chunks
8 yellow cherry tomatoes, quartered
1 whole roasted chicken, deboned & cut into chunks
6 tbsp extra virgin olive oil
1 tbsp Kosher Salt, or an infused salt like garlic-rosemary salt
1 & 1/2 cups finely grated parmiggiano reggiano
Fresh cracked pepper

1. Cook pasta in liberally salted water until 'al dente' firmness (Italian for 'to the tooth', meaning not overcooked; still having some bite/texture to it). Drain
2. When the pasta is about half cooked, add the butter to a large deep pan over medium heat, and melt until it just starts to foam. Add the garlic and cook for 2 to

3 minutes until fragrant and cooked, but not browned, stirring constantly to avoid burning.

3. Add the zucchini, Roma tomatoes, cherry tomatoes, and the chicken and toss to coat with the butter and garlic.

4. Add the cooked drained pasta, olive oil, kosher salt, and 1 cup of the parmesan. Toss together thoroughly and serve immediately, garnished with the remaining 1/2 cup of the parmesan and lots of fresh cracked pepper. Buon Appetito!

Makes 6 large portions

Salt & Pepper Pita Chips

1 package pita bread—pocket style
Olive oil
Salt and fresh cracked pepper

1. Preheat oven to 450 degrees.
2. With a sharp knife, separate the top and bottom halves from each pita pocket to create 2 rounds from each bread.
3. Brush both sides of the rounds with olive oil.
4. Cut each round in half and then each half into 4 equal pie shaped chips. Place these chips on a baking sheet and dust with salt and fresh cracked pepper.
5. Bake for approximately 4 to 6 minutes until mostly golden brown. You may want to rotate the pans half way through the baking time.

11

How to Choose the Perfect Wok

Wok cooking is obviously very popular for Asian dishes, but it can also be used for a wide variety of recipes. One may wonder what makes a wok different from an ordinary pan, and how do I choose the best one?

Just like standard pots and pans, there are just as many different woks on the market to choose from. The recognizable shape of the wok is known worldwide, and this unique shape serves an important purpose. The inner cooking surface, mainly up the sides, should not be smooth. Having rough and/or a slightly uneven surface helps to hold cooked food while the sauce is finished, or other ingredients are being cooked, in the center of the pan. Classic original woks are made out of carbon steel and hammered out by hand, and the residual indentations serve as the perfect surface to assist in doing this.

The round bottoms of the wok also aid in deep frying because it takes less oil to create a deep environment than a regular pot or pan. If you have an electric stove, you may choose to purchase a flat-bottomed wok, but even better would be to purchase a metal wok ring that sits over your electric burner and cradles a round bottom.

Unless you're always cooking for just one or two people, you will get more value out of a larger wok than a smaller one, so buy one slightly larger than you may first think. A larger wok will help to keep the food contained more easily and can be used for both small dinners as well as large. The other thing to consider, before making your purchase however, would be to ensure that you have ample storage for your new wok. Overhead pot racks are especially handy for this predicament.

I don't find that non-stick or electric woks are the best option. Non stick coatings are almost always smooth, there are health concerns about emitting gases from non-stick coatings over high heat, and they don't last as long as they should. Electric woks, I find, don't heat up enough. For traditional high heat wok cooking, one needs to be aware that many pots and pans on the market will also warp over high heat. Make sure you read the manufacturers use recommendations before purchasing to be certain. This being said, one should take care to never submerse any hot pan into water for the same reason.

Although it may be difficult to find one that is hammered out by hand, I do recommend buying a carbon steel wok and seasoning it to create a natural non-stick surface over time. They may not be as pretty to look at, but usually are of the least expensive options. They conduct heat very well, and will last you a lifetime if taken care of properly. Always hand wash only (no soap or scouring pads as they will remove the seasoned surface) and dry thoroughly to prevent rusting. If you insist on buying a non-stick wok, there are cast aluminum options that are non-stick and designed to resist warping.

Accessories that you may consider purchasing for your wok would be a lid, curved bottom utensils, bamboo steamers, hand held wire strainer, and a bamboo scrubber for cleaning. To season your new carbon steel wok, wash with soap and a scrub brush, dry thoroughly, and place the wok over high heat. When it is very hot and the steel has changed colour, turn the heat to medium-low, add a tablespoon of oil, and use a compacted paper towel held with tongs to coat the entire cooking surface with the oil. Let it sit on the medium low heat for approximately 10 to 15 minutes. Allow the wok to cool and repeat as many as three times. This "seasoning" process is only meant for carbon steel woks, not stainless steel or other types of woks.

Dear Chef Dez:
I am a very busy mom/wife and need some fast meal options. Any suggestions?
Diane W.
Abbotsford, BC

Dear Diane,
A great meal solution may be to try wok cooking. It is very fast because of the high heat used and if using a large enough size, dinners can mostly be a one pan meal chocked full of nutritious vegetables. Take a cooking class or watch on-line videos if you are unfamiliar with all the applications of using a wok in the kitchen and also to learn some great nutritious recipes.

Beef & Broccoli Stir-Fry

"A classic Chinese favourite"

600g flank steak
Pepper
4 tbsp grape seed oil or canola oil
8 cups broccoli florets
1 small onion sliced thin
6 cloves garlic, minced
1 to 2 tbsp minced ginger
1/2 cup water
2 cups beef broth
1/2 cup oyster sauce
1/4 cup soy sauce
2.5 to 3 tbsp cornstarch mixed with the soy sauce above
Cooked rice or noodles, optional

1. Slice the flank steak into 3 equal pieces by <u>cutting with the grain</u> of the meat. Then slice each piece <u>against the grain</u> into thin slices on the bias (hold knife at a 45 degree angle instead of straight down). Season the beef slices with pepper.
2. Heat a large wok over high heat.
3. When hot, add 1 tbsp of the oil and sauté half of the beef until juices have evaporated and beef has browned. Remove the beef and set aside. Add another tbsp of oil and repeat with the second half of the beef and set aside.
4. Turn down the heat to medium-high and add the last 2 tbsp of oil. Immediately add the broccoli, onion, garlic, and ginger and sauté for only 30 seconds to ensure the garlic doesn't burn. Add the water and then cover to steam for 2 minutes.
5. Return the beef and any accumulated juices to the wok along with the beef broth, oyster sauce, and soy sauce/cornstarch mixture. Stir together and then move the beef and broccoli up the sides of the wok and boil the sauce in the middle until thickened. Stir everything back together and serve immediately with or without the optional rice/noodles.

Makes approximately 6 full portions

Chicken Shanghai Chow Mein

"If you don't have a wok, a large pan will work just fine"

454g (1 pound) boneless, skinless chicken thighs
454g (1 pound) fresh shanghai noodles
3 tbsp grape seed oil, or peanut oil
3 cloves garlic, chopped
1 tbsp fresh ginger, minced or grated
1 & 1/2 cups shredded cabbage (savoy or sui choy)
1 & 1/2 cups bean sprouts
3 to 4 shitake mushrooms, stems discarded, sliced
1 bunch green onions, sliced into 1-inch lengths
1 small carrot, grated
5 tbsp hoisin sauce
5 tbsp black bean sauce
1/2 cup chicken broth
1/2 tsp sambal oelek
1 to 2 tbsp sesame oil
Soy sauce to season, if desired

1. Slice the chicken thighs into thin strips and set aside.
2. Boil the shanghai noodles until they have separated from each other, then drain and rinse with cold water until cooled. Let drain while preparing recipe.
3. Heat a wok over medium-high to high heat. Add 1 tbsp oil and then approximately one third of the chicken. Cook through until slightly browned. Remove from wok and repeat two more times with remaining oil and chicken.
4. Put all the cooked chicken back into the hot wok. Add the garlic, ginger, cabbage, bean sprouts, mushrooms, green onions, and carrot. Sauté for two or three minutes.
5. Stir in the drained noodles. Add the hoisin sauce, black bean sauce, chicken broth, sambal, and sesame oil. Stir until thoroughly coated and warmed through.
6. Season with soy sauce to taste, if desired.

Makes 4 to 6 portions

Mexican Chipotle Papaya Pork

Originally prepared for Lepp Farm Market www.leppfarmmarket.com
Full colour photo available at www.chefdez.com

"The chunks of sweet papaya adds a wonderful contrast to the smoky heat of the chipotle peppers"

2 pork tenderloins, approximately 600g total
4 tbsp grape seed oil, or canola oil
Salt & Pepper
1 medium onion, chopped
6 garlic cloves, chopped
1 tbsp canned green chillies
1-2 canned chipotle peppers
2 tsp Mexican chilli powder
1 tsp salt
1/4 cup chicken broth
1 medium/large red bell pepper, diced half inch
1 tbsp sugar
1 cup whipping cream
1/4 cup finely chopped cilantro
Juice of 1/2 lime
1/2 Caribbean Red Papaya, cubed large, (approximately 2 cups)
Cooked rice

1. Cube the tenderloins by cutting them in half lengthwise, and then cut into one half inch pieces. Toss the pork chunks with 2 tbsp of the oil and season with some salt and pepper.
2. Heat a large pan over medium high heat. Once hot, add the other 2 tbsp of the oil and then cook the pork until browned and just cooked through, stirring occasionally, approximately 5 to 6 minutes. Remove the pork with a slotted spoon and set aside.
3. Turn the heat to medium. Add the onion, garlic, green chillies, chipotle peppers, chilli powder, and salt. Stir together and cook, stirring occasionally for approximately 2 to 3 minutes.

4. Add the chicken broth and stir to lift off all the flavours from the pan.
5. Stir in the reserved pork (and any pork juices), red pepper, and the sugar.
6. Stir in the cream and reduce over medium high heat until thickened, approximately 2 to 3 minutes.
7. Remove from the heat and stir in the cilantro and lime juice. Season to taste with more salt and pepper if desired.
8. Stir in the papaya chunks and serve immediately with cooked rice.

Makes approximately 4 to 6 portions

Spicy 'Peach & Heat' Pork on Rice

"A great recipe with lots of sauce—perfect on rice! Adjust the amount sambal oelek for the heat intensity you enjoy."

680g (1.5 pounds) pork tenderloins
Salt & pepper
4 tbsp grape seed oil or canola oil
1.5 cups large diced onion
1 cup sliced celery, cut on an angle
1 cup thin sliced carrot, cut on an angle
6 garlic cloves, finely chopped
1 tsp salt
1 to 2 tbsp sambal oelek
1 cup peach jam
2-398ml cans sliced peaches in juice, drained, peaches and 1 cup of juice reserved
1 cup chicken broth
3 tbsp cornstarch, dissolved in a few tbsp of the chicken broth
Cooked rice
Angle cut sliced green onions, for garnish

1. Cut the pork tenderloins in half lengthwise, and then cut into approximately half-inch chunks. Toss the pork chunks with salt & pepper and 2 tbsp of the oil.
2. Heat a wok over medium-high heat and once hot, add the other 2 tbsp of oil to the wok. Fry the pork in small batches until browned, removing with a slotted spoon and setting aside each batch.
3. Add the onion, celery, carrot, garlic and the 1 tsp salt to the wok. Stir fry for 1 minute.
4. Add the reserved pork (and any remaining juices from the pork) and the sambal oelek. Stir fry for 2 to 3 minutes more.
5. Stir in the peach jam. Add the 1 cup of reserved juice, chicken broth, and the dissolved cornstarch mixture. Heat over high heat until boiling and sauce has thickened.
6. Remove from the heat, stir in the reserved peach slices and serve immediately on cooked rice. Garnish with the green onion.

Makes approximately 4 to 6 full portions

12

Benefits of using Zest from Citrus Fruits

There are obviously many benefits gained from using the freshest of ingredients possible when cooking, and using the zest from citrus fruits is no exception. Whether you are using limes, lemons, oranges, or grapefruit, the zest from these fruits will not only add an abundance of flavor as an ingredient, but also create a decorative garnish if you choose.

I will always remember eating peeled oranges as a child and they still had large pieces of the white part of the peel attached to them and tasted very bitter. This is normal. The pale underside of the peel of any citrus is called the pith. It is always more bitter tasting than the flesh of the fruit or the outer coloured part of the peel, called the zest.

There are many ways to include zest as an ingredient. A seafood dish, for example, will always benefit from the addition of lemon zest. Lemon and seafood are a classic combination. Limes are often used in salsas and Mexican cooking so their zest will also enhance many of these types of recipes. Basically a rule of thumb would be to use zest in any recipe that already has citrus juice as an ingredient. This being said, the flavor of an orange chicken stir-fry will taste more complete with addition of orange zest added as an ingredient in the recipe or as a garnish on top of the finished dish. Also because of the natural sweetness of citrus fruits, zest will compliment many desserts as well. Imagine a piece of spiced pumpkin cake topped with a dollop of whipped cream, delicate curls of bright yellow lemon zest, a vibrant green mint leaf, and a sprinkle of cinnamon.

As a garnish, zest will brighten up the appearance of the final plating of your recipe, but should almost always be married up with other contrasting colours. In the cake example above we paired the yellow lemon zest with a green mint leaf and the warm rusty colour of cinnamon. For the orange chicken stir-fry I mentioned, use the orange zest, but maybe some thin diagonal slices of green onion as well. Your imagination is your playground in the kitchen and you should experiment as much as possible to bring enjoyment and attractiveness to the table.

There are basically three ways to remove zest from citrus fruits. Using a knife is one of them but it is not the most effective way, as you always run more of a risk of removing the bitter white pith as well. You are better off using a micro-plane grater or a zester.

Micro-plane graters are the ones being used most on TV cooking shows lately. They are small, long graters with very fine teeth. When placed across the top of a bowl and the citrus fruit is rubbed on it, the bowl will capture the fine gratings of the zest. The downside of using one of these graters is that one always runs the risk of grating too far and getting the white bitter pith as well.

I find zesters are a much better tool. It is a small handheld tool that has five little circular blades at one end. When it is dragged across a citrus fruit from top to bottom, it produces beautiful curls of zest while leaving the bitter pith behind. The obvious benefit of using a zester is for the long curls that are perfect for garnishing. The downside however, would be that if using zest as an ingredient you would then have a second step of chopping. If you currently do not own either tool, I would recommend buying a zester instead of a grater. The zester is less expensive, gives you garnishing versatility and chances are if you are cooking, you already have a knife and cutting board out, so chopping the zest for an ingredient is not as much of a chore as you may first think.

Whichever tool you choose, please remember that you usually get what you pay for. Don't expect a zester purchased for one dollar to work very well. Buying premium kitchen tools are an investment into the health and enjoyment of home cooked meals. When taken care of properly they will last you a lifetime and thus be well worth the money you paid.

Crème Caramel

"My favorite dessert"

2/3 cup sugar
1/3 cup water
1/4 tsp salt

2 cups whipping cream
1 cup milk
1 tsp vanilla extract or vanilla bean paste
1/2 tsp salt
One 2-inch strip of lemon zest
3 large eggs
3 large egg yolks
1/2 cup sugar

1. Preheat oven to 350 degrees Fahrenheit and grease 6 ramekins with butter.
2. Put the 2/3 cup sugar, 1/3 cup water and 1/4 tsp salt in a small heavy bottomed saucepan over medium/low heat until the sugar dissolves. When it starts to turn

brown, swirl in the pan but do not stir until it turns dark rich brown, but not burnt. Immediately pour equal amounts into the prepared ramekins.

3. In another heavy bottomed saucepan, bring the whipping cream, milk, vanilla, salt and the lemon zest to just below a simmer over medium heat. Turn off the heat and let sit while preparing the eggs in the next step.

4. Whisk the 3 whole eggs with the 3 extra egg yolks and the 1/2 cup sugar until frothy.

5. Remove the zest from the cream mixture. Very slowly drizzle the hot cream mixture into the egg mixture while whisking constantly. Doing it slow will prevent the eggs from curdling.

6. Pour this prepared custard mixture into the caramel lined ramekins.

7. Place the filled ramekins into a large pan. Pour boiling water into the pan until the water level reaches approximately half-way up the sides of the ramekins.

8. Carefully put this pan into the oven and reduce the temperature to 325 degrees Fahrenheit. Bake for approximately 40 minutes or until the centers of the custards are almost set (cooked).

9. Refrigerate for a minimum of 2 hours and up to 2 days.

10. To Serve: Loosen the custard in each ramekin by running a butter knife all around the edge of the custard. Invert a plate over the ramekin. Quickly flip the ramekin/plate over and gently jiggle until the custard/caramel come loose. Remove the ramekin and serve on the plate.

Makes 6 portions

Fire Roasted Corn & Black Bean Salsa

Originally prepared for Lepp Farm Market www.leppfarmmarket.com
Full colour photo available at www.chefdez.com

"Fantastic accompaniment at your next BBQ—great on grilled steak, chicken, and fish . . . or serve it as an appetizer with your favourite tortilla chips"

2 cobs sweet corn, husks removed
1 large red bell pepper, cut into large pieces
1 medium red onion, sliced thick
2 tbsp canola oil
1/2 cup rinsed and drained canned black beans
1/4 cup soft sundried tomatoes, finely chopped
1/4 cup firmly packed finely chopped fresh cilantro
2 garlic cloves, crushed
Zest of 1 lime, finely chopped
Juice of 1 lime
1/2 tsp salt
1/4 tsp fresh cracked pepper

1. Preheat your grill until hot.
2. Toss the corn, red pepper, and onion with the canola oil to coat.
3. Grill until mostly charred. Let cool.
4. Cut the corn kernels off the cobs, and chop the red pepper and onion into small pieces. Transfer all to a medium sized bowl.
5. Stir in the remaining ingredients and serve!

Makes approximately 4 cups

Lemon Soufflés

"If you love the flavour of lemon, you will love this dessert"

Butter for the dishes
2 tbsp butter
1 & 1/4 cups sugar
7 tbsp flour
1/2 tsp baking powder
1/4 tsp salt
4 large eggs, whites and yolks separated
2 tsp grated lemon zest
1/2 cup fresh lemon juice
1 cup milk

1. Preheat oven to 300 degrees. Butter a 5-6 small ramekins. Place them in a large pan that will allow them to be baked bain-marie style (surrounded by boiling water).
2. In a med-large mixing bowl, cream the 2 tbsp butter with the 3/4 cup of the sugar. Stir in the flour, baking powder, and salt.
3. In a separate bowl beat the egg whites to moist peaks, and then whip in the remaining 1/2 cup sugar until just mixed.
4. Beat the egg yolks. Add the egg yolks, zest, lemon juice, and milk to the dry ingredients. Fold in the whipped egg whites. Immediately pour into dishes.
5. Add boiling water to the bain-marie and bake for 55 to 60 minutes until golden brown and set. Let cool slightly on rack and then serve warm or room temperature.

Makes 5 to 6 portions

Marinated Chicken with Garlic Quinoa

"Quinoa (pronounced 'keen-wah') is a great grain that is lower in carbohydrates and higher in protein."

2/3 cup olive oil
1/3 cup fresh lemon juice, zest from the lemons reserved
1 tbsp white wine vinegar
6 garlic cloves, crushed
1 tbsp dried oregano leaves
1 tbsp dried basil leaves
Salt and pepper to season
6 boneless/skinless chicken breast halves
2 tbsp canola oil
6 garlic cloves, chopped
2 cups quinoa
4 cups water
1 tsp salt
1/2 tsp pepper

1. Mix the oil, lemon juice, vinegar, garlic, oregano, and basil in a large bowl. Season to taste with salt & pepper—season it as if you were making a salad dressing.
2. Add the chicken and marinate in fridge for 3-4 hours, tossing occasionally.
3. Remove the chicken from the marinade and grill over a medium to medium-high heat until done, approximately 10-20 minutes depending on the temperature of your grill. Alternatively, bake in a 400 degree oven for approximately 20 minutes.
4. While the chicken is cooking prepare the quinoa—add the 2 tbsp oil and chopped garlic to a pot and cook briefly over medium heat—make sure to not burn the garlic otherwise it will taste bitter. Stir in the quinoa and cook for another 30 seconds. Add the water, salt & pepper and continue to cook on medium to medium-high heat uncovered, stirring occasionally, until all of the liquid has been absorbed/evaporated, approximately 15 to 20 minutes. Re-season to taste if necessary.
5. Serve a mound of quinoa topped with the chicken breast, and garnish with the reserved lemon zest.

Makes 6 portions

Marinated Olives

2 cups drained kalamata olives
2 cups drained green olives
1 cup extra virgin olive oil
5 anchovy filets, chopped fine
1/4 cup chopped fresh rosemary
1/4 cup chopped fresh thyme
1/4 cup fresh lemon juice, zest reserved
2 tbsp minced onion
2 tbsp minced garlic
2 tbsp fennel seeds
1 tsp fresh cracked pepper
Finely minced lemon zest from above
3 tbsp balsamic vinegar

1. Combine and mix all of the ingredients except for the balsamic. Cover and chill for 8 hours or up to 3 days.
2. Bring to room temperature. Remove with a slotted spoon and stir in the balsamic vinegar.

Strawberry Margarita Soy Dessert

Full colour photo available at www.chefdez.com

"This small dessert can also be served as a palate cleanser between courses. It is very simple and brings together the flavours of a refreshing strawberry margarita together with your sweetened soy dessert. Plated beautifully, it makes a wonderful addition to any summer meal."

8-10 fresh strawberries, sliced thin
5-6 tsp tequila
3 tsp sugar
Zest from 2 limes, chopped fine
1-300g package sweetened tofu soy dessert

1. Gently toss the strawberries, tequila, sugar and lime zest together in a bowl and set aside.
2. Cut the soy dessert into 8 equal portions (cut in half and then each half into four). Pull a fine kitchen string or thread through to make perfect slices as it is very delicate.
3. Plate individually on 8 small plates: 1 cut portion of soy dessert topped with equal amounts of the strawberry tequila mixture.

Makes 8 small portions

13
Breakfast Ideas

On many occasions I have mentioned great ways to transform your dinner making experience into a special event, like pouring a glass of wine and putting on some great music, but what about breakfast? Isn't this the most important meal of the day? Yes, to most health professionals it is, so this column is dedicated to making that pinnacle feast into something extraordinary.

I understand that a vast percentage of the population have "day jobs" and that making a spectacular breakfast on a weekday is far from being at the top of your priority list. These ideas are more geared towards your days off or if you work evenings.

This is the perfect circumstance to forget about the bowl of cold cereal or toast and jam, and blow the dust off some old cookbooks to try something new. One of my wife's favorite breakfast pastimes is making and perfecting different pancake recipes from around the world. It seems that every walk of life has their own version of what we know as the traditional North American pancake. Making it a tradition to do a different pancake recipe every Saturday or Sunday morning is a fantastic journey around the culinary world.

French toast is another common "special" breakfast that many people enjoy, but we prepare it differently on many instances. Instead of the traditional method of dipping bread in batter and frying in a pan, we often will make a large casserole dish of French toast the night before, letting the egg mixture soak in, and then baking it the next morning. Not only is it an extraordinary display at the breakfast table, it also allows us to have more free time in the morning to sip our special coffees and enjoy each other's company.

Actually there are many recipes that you can get mostly prepared the night before, like muffins or biscuits for example. Measure and combine all of the dry ingredients and then all you have to do is incorporate the wet ingredients in the morning.

Incorporating fresh baked breads or unique types of bread will also enhance an ordinary breakfast. One way to make this easy is to prep the loaf the evening before, cover with plastic wrap and store in the refrigerator overnight. The bread might rise slightly in the fridge, but you will need to remove it from the fridge an hour or two before baking. Remove the plastic wrap, let it rise in a warm place until it doubles its original size and bake as usual. On many occasions we will serve fresh baked bread simply topped with butter and honey.

If all of this seems like "work" however, there is one very quick way to help transform your regular breakfast of cold cereal: top with a handful of fresh in-season berries or some slices of banana. This will take very little time, offer more flavor and nutrition, and make a better presentation. There is a reason why all the photos of cereal on the cereal boxes are like this: better presentation equals more of a chance of you buying it.

Dear Chef Dez:

I love pancakes, but whenever I make them they turn out tough. I know it's not the recipe because it is the same one that my mom uses and hers always turn out fluffy and delicate. Can you help me?

Sarah D.
Burnaby, BC

Dear Sarah:

Pancakes are much like quick breads as they should have a cake-like texture, hence the name pan-"cakes." The biggest mistake made when preparing pancake batter is that one tends to over-mix. Over-mixing flour and liquid produces gluten, which will give it more structure. The more mixing one does, the more gluten is created, and the tougher the cooked pancakes will be. It is okay for your batter to be a bit lumpy. The lumps won't be evident in the cooked pancake.

Also, make sure you are not using "bread" flour, as it contains more gluten than all-purpose or pastry flour. I hope this helps.

Baked Apple French Toast

Recipe created by Katherine Desormeaux (Mrs. Chef Dez)

"A great make-ahead breakfast"

12 slices of bread
Butter for the pan
5 tbsp butter
3 tbsp brown sugar
4 apples, peeled & diced
1 tsp cinnamon
1/4 white wine or apple juice
1 tbsp cornstarch
5 large eggs
1 & 1/2 cups milk
1/4 cup sugar
1 tsp vanilla extract
1 tsp salt

1. Trim bread slices to fit in a 9 x 13 inch glass casserole dish (6 slices by 2 layers sandwich style). Remove the bread slices and set aside. Butter the pan and arrange a single layer of the bread back in the pan.
2. Melt 2 tbsp of the butter in a pan with the brown sugar over medium heat. Add the apples and cinnamon and cook until the apples are soft. In a small bowl mix the wine (or apple juice) with the cornstarch and add it to the cooked apples. Bring to a boil to thicken. Remove from heat and let cool slightly.
3. Spread cooked apple mixture evenly over the single bread layer. Arrange the second layer of bread slices over the apple mixture.
4. In a bowl, beat the eggs. Whisk in the milk, sugar, vanilla and salt until thoroughly combined. Pour over the bread/apples. Leave to soak for 1/2 hour or cover and refrigerate overnight.
5. Break the remaining 3 tbsp butter into small bits and sprinkle over the top and sprinkle with some more cinnamon. Bake for approximately 40 to 50 minutes in a

preheated 350 degree Fahrenheit oven, until egg mixture has cooked. Let stand 10 minutes before serving.

Makes 6 portions

Breakfast Focaccia Bread

Recipe created by Katherine Desormeaux (Mrs. Chef Dez)

"This dish can be made with 6 apples <u>or</u> with 2 cups pecans. Alternatively it can be made with both: 3 apples and 1 cup pecans together."

1 & 3/4 cups water
2 tbsp vegetable or canola oil
2 & 1/2 cups all-purpose flour
2 cups whole wheat flour
1/4 cup white sugar
2 tsp salt
2 tsp cinnamon
3 & 1/2 tsp quick rise yeast

6 tbsp butter
3/4 cup dark brown sugar
2 tbsp whipping cream
Pinch of salt
2 to 3 tsp cinnamon
3 to 6 apples, peeled, cored, and sliced thin
And/Or
1 to 2 cups pecan halves

1. Prepare a 12 inch x 17 inch jelly roll pan with baking spray.
2. Add the water, oil, both flours, white sugar, 2 tsp salt, 2 tsp cinnamon, and the yeast to a bread machine and use the "dough" setting to prepare the bread dough. Or alternatively you can prepare as usual for making bread dough from scratch.
3. In a heavy bottomed pot, melt the butter, brown sugar, cream, and salt. Bring to a boil, reduce heat and simmer 1 minute. Pour into the prepared jelly roll pan and spread as evenly as possible. Sprinkle with the 2 to 3 tsp cinnamon. Arrange the pecans and/or apple slices over this sugar cinnamon layer (if using both, apples & pecans, put the pecans on the pan first).
4. On a floured surface, roll the prepared bread dough to the approximate size of the jelly roll pan. Fold the dough to facilitate moving it to the pan, and then unfold to fit the pan and arranging it carefully on the apple/pecan layer, pressing it into place.
5. At this point the focaccia can be dusted lightly with flour, covered with plastic wrap, and placed in the refrigerator overnight. In the morning, remove it to a warm, draft free place (I put it in the oven with the light on for warmth) for 1 to 1.5 hours until doubled in thickness. If you do not choose to do the overnight method, the bread should only need to rise for 45 to 60 minutes.
6. Bake at 350 degrees Fahrenheit for 20 to 25 minutes until golden brown and cooked through.
7. Cool 10 minutes then carefully flip the bread over onto a large cutting board. Cut the bread into 12 equal pieces, and then cut each rectangle in half diagonally to create 24 triangle shaped pieces. Serve warm with butter.

Makes 24 pieces

Nana's Sweet Milk Pancakes

Thanks to Bonnie Swanson for this family favorite recipe for basic pancakes

2 cups flour
2 tbsp sugar
4 tsp baking powder
1 tsp salt
2 large eggs, beaten
3 tbsp melted butter
2 cups milk

1. In a large bowl combine all of the dry ingredients (flour, sugar, baking powder and salt).
2. In a separate bowl, combine the wet ingredients (eggs, butter and nilk).
3. Add the wet ingredients into the dry ingredients and mix until just combined—DO NOT OVERMIX.
4. With a large ladle, pour a portion of the batter onto a hot pan. Once bubbles form and start to pop on the surface of the pancakes, flip over to cook the other side until golden brown.

Berry Pancakes

Using the recipe above, in each ladle full on pancake batter when freshly put in the hot pan, quickly arrange a number of fresh or frozen berries (blueberries, raspberries, blackberries, cut strawberries, etc) in each round. Cook as normal but using more care when it comes to flipping.

Fruit Pancakes

Using the recipe above, and the same technique as the Berry Pancakes, add any small diced soft fresh fruit you desire (such as peaches, bananas, etc).

Pannekoeken

Recipe created by Katherine Desormeaux (Mrs. Chef Dez)

"Also known as Dutch pancakes and they are one of our family favorites"

4 large eggs
1 & 3/4 cups milk
1 & 1/2 cups flour
2 tbsp sugar
1/2 tsp salt
1 tsp quick rise yeast
Butter for the pan
Butter, fruit, syrup, and whipped cream for serving

1. Place all ingredients in a blender or food processor and mix at high speed for 1 to 2 minutes. Alternatively, whisk eggs and milk together until mostly combined. Measure in flour, sugar, salt, and yeast on top and whisk in all together until smooth.
2. Allow batter to sit for 1 hour to overnight.
3. Heat a large non-stick pan over medium heat and grease lightly with butter. Pour 2 to 4 tbsp of batter into the pan and tip and swirl until the batter covers the bottom of the pan. When the batter appears to be partly cooked right to the middle (approximately 1 minute), use a spatula or silicone scraper to loosen the edges and carefully flip the pannekoeken. Remove when cooked and continue until all the batter is used up, stacking them to help keep warm.
4. For serving, fold each pannekoeken into quarters and serve with butter, your favorite fresh or canned fruit, syrup and whipped cream

Pumpkin Pancakes

Recipe created by Katherine Desormeaux (Mrs. Chef Dez)

"The taste of pumpkin pie in pancakes"

2 cups all-purpose flour
2 tbsp sugar
1 tbsp baking powder
1 & 1/2 tsp ground cinnamon
1 tsp salt
1/4 tsp ground nutmeg
1/4 tsp ground cloves
1/4 tsp ground ginger
2 large eggs, beaten
2 & 1/4 cups milks, or 2 & 1/2 cups buttermilk
1/2 cup pumpkin puree
2 tbsp vegetable oil or canola oil

1. Combine the flour, sugar, baking powder, cinnamon, salt, nutmeg, cloves, and ginger in a large mixing bowl.
2. In a separate smaller bowl, combine the eggs, milk or buttermilk, pumpkin and oil together.
3. Preheat a non-stick pan or griddle over medium heat.
4. Pour the wet ingredients into the dry ingredients and mix until just combined—DO NOT OVERMIX.
5. With a large ladle, pour a portion of the batter onto the hot pan. Once bubbles form and start to pop on the surface of the pancakes, flip over to cook the other side until golden brown.

Makes approximately 12 to 14 four-inch pancakes.

Wealth Cakes

Recipe created by Katherine Desormeaux (Mrs. Chef Dez)

"My twist on classic Welsh Cakes. Our son Noah started calling them "wealth cakes" and the name has since become customary in our home."

2 cups whole wheat flour
1/2 cup white sugar
2 tsp baking powder
1 tsp ground cinnamon
1/2 tsp salt
1/2 tsp ground nutmeg
1/4 tsp ground cloves
1/2 cup butter, very cold or frozen
1/2 cup currants
1/4 tsp finely grated lemon zest
1/3 cup milk
1 large egg
More butter and cinnamon sugar for serving

1. In a large bowl mix the flour, sugar, baking powder, cinnamon, salt, nutmeg, and cloves together. With a medium grater, grate the butter into this flour mixture and stir in (alternatively cut the butter in as for pastry). Stir in the currants and lemon zest.
2. Make a well in the center of the mixture. Add the milk and crack the egg into the milk. Beat the egg until reasonably mixed with the milk and then incorporate into the dry mixture to form a dough. DO NOT OVER MIX.
3. Roll or pat on a floured surface to about 2cm thick and cut into small circles.
4. Fry on both sides in a non-stick pan over medium to medium-low heat until brown on both sides and cooked through, approximately 3 to 5 minutes per side.
5. Dip hot cakes into a cinnamon sugar mixture and serve with butter.

Makes 24 small cakes depending on the size of round cutter

Yeasty Biscuits

Recipe created by Katherine Desormeaux (Mrs. Chef Dez)

2 tsp fast acting yeast
1/4 cup warm water
4 cups all-purpose flour
4 tsp baking powder
3 tbsp sugar
1 tsp salt
1/2 cup very cold or frozen butter
1 & 1/4 cups milk

1. Preheat oven to 400 degrees Fahrenheit.
2. In a two cup glass measure, dissolve yeast in the water and set aside.
3. In a separate bowl mix the flour, baking powder, sugar, and salt together. Grate in the cold butter with a medium sized grater and stir to distribute.
4. Add the milk to the yeast mixture. Add this wet mixture to the flour mixture. Stir and knead just until smooth. Shape the dough into a rectangle approximately 1.5cm to 2cm thick. Cut into 12 equal sized biscuits.
5. Prepare a baking sheet with baking spray or parchment paper. Arrange the biscuits on the baking sheet, cover with a clean towel and allow to rise for 20 minutes on top of the stove while pre-heating oven to 400 degrees.
6. Bake for 12 to 15 minutes.

Makes 12 biscuits

Quick Cinnamon Rolls

Recipe created by Katherine Desormeaux (Mrs. Chef Dez)

"Much quicker than traditional yeast raised cinnamon buns, and just as tasty!"

1 recipe of Yeasty Biscuits (above)
1/2 cup room temperature butter
1/2 cup firmly packed brown sugar
3 tsp cinnamon

1. Prepare the dough as mentioned in the Yeasty Biscuits recipe, but instead roll the dough into an approximate 25cm x 60cm rectangle.
2. Use 1 tbsp of the room temperature butter to liberally grease a 9x13 inch cake pan. Spread the remaining room temperature butter evenly over the rectangle of dough, leaving 2cm on the long edge without butter (to seal the roll). Spread the brown sugar evenly over the butter and sprinkle with the cinnamon.
3. Roll up the dough in a jelly roll fashion and cut into 12 equal pieces. Arrange in the prepared pan, cover with a clean towel and allow to rise for 20 minutes on top of the stove while pre-heating oven to 400 degrees.
4. Bake for 12 to 15 minutes.

Makes 12 cinnamon rolls

14
Pasta Sauce Ideas

In previous columns I have suggested on a number of occasions that one should try their hand at making fresh pasta instead of always relying on purchasing it dry from a bag or box. Congratulations to you if you took my advice and tried your hand at this wonderful culinary skill. For those of you that did, and for those of you that never will, I want to give you some ideas for sauces to compliment your pasta, be it from fresh or dry.

The most common is the classic tomato sauce. Although Chefs will consider it sacrilege to any pasta, a number of people still buy canned or jarred premade tomato sauces to don their pasta. Some will at least get creative by adding extra ingredients like onions or garlic, but nothing can take the place of good rustic homemade batch of tomato sauce. This does not have to be the style that simmers for hours on end either. Many great homemade pasta sauces can start out with a little help from canned diced tomatoes and some tomato paste and be done in record time. Reduce it down even further at the end (by simmering some of the water content out) and replenish with some whipping cream and you now have a rosé sauce for those special occasions when calorie counting is not on your priority list.

Any ground meat (beef, pork, chicken, turkey, lamb, etc) cooked up at the beginning of the process will magically transform this rustic tomato or rosé sauce into a hearty meat sauce. Sausage meat can also be utilized in the same manner by removing it from the casings and cooking the same as ground meat. Italian sausage (mild or hot, depending on your tastes) is wonderful for this.

A béchamel (white sauce) is a very simple sauce. Don't let the fancy French culinary name scare you—it's just milk thickened with flour and butter. A little seasoning (salt, pepper, and a pinch of ground nutmeg) and you have an incredible sauce that can be a blank canvas for your favorite cheeses to be melted in or tossed with bits of grilled chicken. Add garlic and parmesan and you will basically have alfredo sauce.

Oils infused with flavors and seasonings can be the base of a tasty light pasta coating. Heating olive oil over medium to low heat and letting ingredients like crushed garlic, chillies, herbs, etc. infuse their way into transforming a ordinary oil into a savoury enhancement. These types of sauces are perfect for less filling side dishes or during hot weather when a heavily thickened sauce is not desired.

A batch of seasoned simmered vegetables can also be transformed into a smooth sauce bursting with flavors with the help of a blender, food processor, or hand immersion blender. We actually do one with ground lamb where it is simmered with a number of vegetables and herbs with some red wine. A few good pulses in a blender, at the end of the cook time, alter it into an amazing pasta sauce.

One of the quickest pasta sauces you will ever make is a browned-butter sauce. It is exactly what the name states it to be—butter that has been browned. Take a hot pan and place a handful of cubes of cold butter into it. Stir, or lift the pan and swirl the melting butter, until the butter foam has just started to brown and then toss with your favorite pasta. Your favorite fresh delicate herb (basil, oregano, sage, etc) can also be added at the time of the cold butter for an incredible infusion of herbal essential oils. Although we have all been taught never to add butter to a hot pan for fear that it will burn, the trick is to remove the "browning" butter before it hits the "burning" stage. Use salted butter to be more complimentary in taste and less seasoning you will have to do afterwards.

These are merely suggestions as it would be literally impossible to cover every single type of pasta sauce idea here. What I want this column to be is an invitation for you to blow some dust off your cookbook collection or search recipes from the internet. Pasta is probably my favorite thing to eat, but I realize with most people that eating is not the problem; it's the cooking part that feels like a chore sometimes. Find a way to make it fun. When I was younger, one thing I always insisted on when cooking pasta was to listen to Pavarotti while doing so. I still do on occasion, but now it is not only Pavarotti, but also Andrea Bocelli, Josh Groban and others . . . and always with a glass of wine.

I was told never to rinse my pasta after cooking. Is this right?

Derek C.
Vancouver, BC

Dear Derek,

This is correct for the most part. If serving it right away, rinsing your pasta will not only cool it down, but will also wash away starch. We always want to serve a piping hot meal and the starch helps pasta sauce 'stick' to the pasta. Basically the only time I would rinse pasta is if I needed to cool it down immediately, like preparing a pasta salad for example.

Lamb Pasta Sauce

Full colour photo available at www.chefdez.com

"A pasta sauce for lamb lovers!"

500g lean ground lamb
2 tbsp extra virgin olive oil
1 small onion, diced small
1 carrot, diced small
1 celery stalk, diced small
10 to 15 juniper berries, optional
3 garlic cloves, chopped
1 to 2 fresh rosemary sprigs, stems discarded
1 & 1/2 tsp salt
1/2 tsp pepper
1/2 cup full-bodied red wine, or low-sodium beef broth
2 bay leaves
500g pasta shapes, like penne, rigatoni, etc, cooked as desired
Chopped fresh parsley for garnish

1. Add the lamb, oil, onion, carrot, celery, juniper berries, garlic, rosemary, salt and pepper to a large pan. Cook over medium heat until the lamb is cooked through,

stirring occasionally and breaking up the lamb as it cooks, approximately 10 minutes.

2. Stir in the red wine (or low-sodium beef broth) and the bay leaves. Bring to a boil and then cover, reduce the heat to low and simmer covered for 1 hour.

3. Remove and discard the bay leaves. Pulse the cooked sauce in a blender until a smooth consistency is reached. Re-season to taste with salt & pepper if necessary.

4. Serve immediately on the freshly cooked pasta and garnish with chopped parsley.

Makes approximately 3.5 cups of sauce, or 4 to 6 portions with the cooked pasta

Pasta Carbonara

"Incredibly rich—not for everyday eating, but an outstanding pasta dish to serve on a special occasion!"

1 pound (454g) dry pasta of your choice
250g bacon slices, sliced into 1/4 inch pieces
1 cup frozen peas
1/4 cup small diced onion
4 garlic cloves, minced
1/4 cup white wine
2 large eggs, beaten
1 & 1/2 cups whipping cream
3/4 cup grated parmesan cheese
Salt & Pepper to season

1. Bring a large pot of salted water to a boil and cook the pasta until desired doneness.

2. While waiting for the water to boil, cook the bacon until crisp in a large pan over medium/high heat. When crisp, remove from the heat and carefully stir in the peas. Add the onion, garlic and wine. Stir to combine and still off the heat just let the residual heat from the pan cook the onion and garlic.

3. When the pasta is done cooking, thoroughly drain it and add toss it with the bacon mixture.

4. In a bowl, thoroughly combine the eggs and cream together. Slowly pour this mixture into the pasta while mixing constantly to avoid curdling the eggs. The egg/cream mixture must not boil or it will curdle.

5. Toss in the parmesan and season to taste with salt and fresh cracked pepper.

Dez's Famous Sausage & Fennel Pasta

Originally prepared for Lepp Farm Market www.leppfarmmarket.com
Full colour photo available at www.chefdez.com

3 tbsp olive oil
500g mild Italian sausage, casings removed
1 medium onion, diced very small
4-6 large cloves of garlic, minced
2 tbsp fennel seed
1 tsp salt
A few grinds of black pepper
1-156ml can tomato paste
1-796ml can of diced tomatoes
1 cup of full-bodied red wine
1 tsp vegetable stock paste
2 tbsp white sugar
1/2 tsp sambal oelek, optional
400g penne pasta or other favourite pasta shape
1 cup whipping cream
Chopped fresh parsley, for garnish
Grated Parmigiano Reggiano cheese, for garnish

1. Add the olive oil, sausage, onion, garlic, fennel seed, salt and pepper to a large heavy bottomed pan.

2. Turn the heat on to medium-high and cook, while breaking up the sausage, until the sausage is fully cooked and in small pieces, approximately 8 to 12 minutes.

3. Stir in the tomato paste, diced tomatoes, wine, vegetable paste, sugar, and sambal oelek. Bring to a boil and reduce over medium heat until the sauce becomes very thick, approximately 10 to 15 minutes. Cook your pasta in boiling, liberally salted water to desired consistency (approximately 13 to 15 minutes for penne) during this step.

4. Once the sauce has reduced, stir in the whipping cream and then the cooked and drained pasta. Serve immediately garnished with parsley and grated Parmigiano Reggiano.

Makes approximately 6 portions

Whiskey Shrimp Pasta

"Black Tiger Prawns give this the best flavour"

2 tbsp butter
1 celery stalk, sliced
1 carrot, sliced
4-6 garlic cloves, chopped
1 small onion, chopped
680g prawns with shells, peeled, & shells reserved
Salt & pepper
1/2 cup white wine
2 bay leaves
2 tsp dried tarragon
----
2 tsp canola oil

1 large shallot, sliced thin
1 & 1/4 cups chicken stock
1/4 cup whiskey
3 tbsp tomato paste
1 cup whipping cream
1 tsp salt
1 tsp pepper
1 large red bell pepper, julienne cut
454g dry pasta of your choice, cooked al dente
Chopped parsley, for garnish

1. Place the butter in a large pan over medium heat and when butter starts to foam, add the celery, carrot, garlic, onion, and the shells from the prawns (reserve the prawn meat for later). Season with salt & pepper and cook for 2 to 3 minutes until the vegetables have softened a bit. Add the wine, bay leaves and tarragon and bring to a boil. Cover & simmer for 10 to 15 minutes to bring out the flavour of the prawn shells. Strain and reserve the liquid in a separate container (discard the solids).
2. Put the pan back on the heat; add the canola oil and sauté the shallot for 1 minute.
3. Add 1/4 cup of the chicken stock to deglaze the pan. Carefully add the whiskey and carefully ignite with a long match/lighter. Flambé until the flames subside.
4. Stir in the tomato paste, and then add the remaining 1 cup of chicken stock, the whipping cream, 1 tsp salt, 1 tsp pepper, and the reserved liquid from step 1.
5. Heat over medium high heat and reduce until a thick sauce consistency is reached, stirring frequently. Add the prawn meat and the red pepper and continue stirring until the prawns are just cooked. Re—season if necessary and toss with the cooked pasta.
6. Garnish with chopped parsley & serve immediately.

Makes 4 portions

15

Be Proud of Your Tastes and Level of Food Knowledge

There are people who feel that their food preferences or knowledge may not reflect what is correct or up-to-date in the culinary world. This is completely understandable as there is always an endless supply of information and techniques. This does not commensurate however that one should be ashamed, or be denied of the right, to express their passion for this necessity in our lives.

One of the many things that I love about food and food preparation is that I never stop learning. One can never know everything in this industry and I consider it to be one of "the arts" like music or painting. Never can every musical note and lyric, colour and design, or food flavour combination be "used up". It is literally impossible. No matter how much or little you know, chances are you have preferences in your appreciation of this medium that is both an essential and an indulgent part of our lives. This individuality not only guides you to determine likes or dislikes, but defines you as who you are.

Carving a baron of beef in a buffet line-up at a Hotel many years ago, I was approached by and elderly woman with an empty plate. As always, I asked the level of doneness preferred. Looking nervous, she whispered, "I know it's not the right way, but I prefer an extra well-done piece". So I asked her "what do you enjoy?" and she repeated "extra well-done" with a sense of bewilderment. "If that's what you enjoy," I stated to her "how is that the wrong way?"

Many people lose site of this and in the meantime get blackballed by a definition governed by the Culinary World. The "textbook" doneness for red meat is medium-rare for optimal flavour, juiciness, and tenderness. This is a merely guideline however, and not meant to overrule ones preferences. If you don't enjoy red meat medium-rare, then it is not the right way for you.

As long as one seizes opportunities to try new foods and preparation techniques, then there should be nothing wrong with their final individual evaluation. The culinary world is full of guidelines, but the sooner people realize that these "guidelines" are not necessarily "laws", the better off everyone will be.

> *Dear Chef Dez:*
>
> *Recently I went to a restaurant and ordered a well-done steak. The server advised me that the Chef in the kitchen refused to cook my steak of choice to that degree of doneness. What is your opinion on this?*
>
> *Peter F.*
> *Langley, BC*

> *Dear Peter:*
>
> *Depending on the cut of steak, most restaurants will fulfill your request. Some however feel that for a top grade cut of beef, cooking it well-done is a waste. It just dries out the optimal flavour and tenderness that a choice cut is expected to offer the consumer.*
>
> *I think the situation should have been handled differently. You should have been advised that the kitchen doesn't recommend "well-done" for the selection of steak you made, and offer you a different cut. If at this point you still insisted on your original choice, then your request should have been honoured.*
>
> *I feel as professionals it is our obligation to educate people on the culinary guidelines that we are trained in and to make appropriate suggestions. If, however, the consumer still chooses otherwise, their wish should be respected and their individuality recognized.*

Clam Chowder

Full colour photo available at www.chefdez.com

"Adding tomatoes to this cream based soup gives this classic New England style chowder more flavour and colour"

2 large red skin potatoes, diced 1/2 inch
2 tbsp olive oil
1 tbsp butter
1 medium onion, diced small
4 cloves garlic, minced
1 large carrot, sliced thin
2 large celery stalks, sliced thin
2 tsp dried tarragon
1 tsp dried basil
2 bay leaves
4 to 5 tsp salt
3 tsp sugar
1 & 1/2 tsp pepper
1/2 tsp sambal oelek, optional
1/4 cup flour
2-142g cans clams, clams & liquid separated and set aside
2 & 1/2 cups milk
1 & 1/2 cups whipping cream
2 large tomatoes, diced 1/2 inch
1/4 cup chopped fresh parsley

1. Steam the diced potatoes for approximately 8 to 10 minutes—do not overcook. Set aside.
2. Over medium heat, add the oil and butter to a large pot. Once the butter has melted add the onion, garlic, carrot, celery, tarragon, basil, bay leaves, salt, sugar, pepper, and sambal oelek. Stir to coat, and then cover and cook for approximately 5 minutes,

stirring once during this cooking time. This will 'sweat' the vegetables in their own juice, not brown them.

3. Remove the lid and stir in the flour. Cook for another 2 to 3 minutes to remove the starchy taste of the flour, stirring occasionally.

4. To avoid lumps, stir in the liquid from the cans of clams very slowly. Once added, follow with the milk and whipping cream. Once all the liquid has been combined add the reserved potatoes, reserved clams, and tomatoes. Turn heat to medium-low and continue to cook until the soup is hot and has thickened slightly, stirring frequently to avoid burning.

5. Remove the bay leaves and discard them. Stir in the parsley, and serve immediately.

Makes 6 to 8 portions.

Eggs Benedict with Bacon & Cheese Sauce

"A white cheddar cheese sauce replaces the classic hollandaise sauce to make this recipe a bit more approachable for the Home Chef"

1/4 cup butter
1/4 cup flour
1 & 1/2 to 2 cups milk
2 cups grated white cheddar
1/2 tsp salt
Pinch of ground white pepper
4 large eggs, poached
2 English muffins, split and toasted
6 slices bacon, cooked

1. In a heavy bottomed small saucepan, melt the butter over low heat. Stir in the flour and continue to cook over low heat, stirring occasionally, to cook the starchy taste

out of the flour, approximately 5 to 7 minutes. Add the 1 & 1/2 cups milk very slowly while whisking into the butter/flour mixture. It will get extremely thick at first, but keep working in small amounts of the milk at a time to prevent lumps. Turn the heat to medium once all of the milk has been incorporated. Add the grated cheese and continue to whisk constantly until the mixture thickens and just comes to a boil. If the sauce is too thick then add the extra milk to thin it out. Remove from the heat and set aside. Season with the 1/2 teaspoon of salt and the white pepper.

2. Poach the eggs to desired doneness, toast the muffins, and assemble as follows: per serving place one muffin half, 1 & 1/2 slices bacon, one egg, top with hot cheese sauce, and serve immediately.

Makes four single egg portions

Oven Roasted Root Vegetables

"To prevent excessive bleeding of the red beets into the other vegetables, soak and rinse the diced beets with cold water and then drain thoroughly before using in the recipe"

<u>One heaping cup of 1/2 inch diced of each of the following root vegetables:</u>
Onion
Rutabaga
Turnip
Sweet Potato
Beets
Carrots

2 large sprigs of fresh rosemary, stems discarded
2 tbsp canola oil, vegetable oil, or olive oil
2 tsp salt
1/2 tsp pepper
1 tbsp Maple Syrup

1. Preheat oven to 450 degrees Fahrenheit.
2. In a large bowl toss all of the ingredients together (except for the maple syrup).
3. Spread on a large baking sheet making sure the cut vegetables are not crowded.
4. Bake for 30 minutes, tossing every 5 to 7 minutes.
5. Add the maple syrup and stir to coat. Bake for another 10 minutes.

Makes approximately 5 to 6 cups

Steaks with Merlot Reduction

Originally prepared for Lepp Farm Market www.leppfarmmarket.com
Full colour photo available at www.chefdez.com

"Red wine pan sauces are the quickest path to an incredible tasting steak. You've never had a steak fried in a pan taste so good . . . until now."

2-New York Strip Steaks, approx 12oz each
Salt & pepper
1-2 tsp grape seed oil or canola oil
1/2 tsp beef stock paste
1/2 cup Merlot or other full bodied red wine
1/4 cup whipping cream
1 tsp sugar

1. Pre-heat a heavy bottomed pan over medium-high heat.
2. Season both sides of the steaks with salt and pepper.
3. When the pan is hot, add the oil and then the steaks. Cook for approximately two and one half minutes per side (for a total of 5 minutes) for rare to medium rare (depending on the temperature of the steaks, thickness of the steaks, and temperature of the pan).
4. Remove the steaks from the pan and let them rest.

5. Remove the pan from the heat temporarily and immediately add the beef stock paste and then deglaze with the Merlot.
6. Return the pan to the heat and stir in the whipping cream and sugar.
7. Boil the sauce, stirring constantly until syrupy—checking for consistency by occasionally removing the pan from the heat to let the boiling subside.
8. Pour the sauce immediately over the steaks and serve. If you are not pouring the sauce immediately over the steaks, then transfer the finished sauce to a small serving dish as the residual heat from the pan will continue to evaporate the sauce into an unusable paste.

Makes 2 portions

16

Knife Skills in the Kitchen

Nothing is better than having a personal one-on-one lesson on cutting, but I will try to do my best in written form to communicate some basic tips to get you started.

When holding a "Chef's" knife, it is important to have it balanced properly in your hand to reduce fatigue and improve control. To find this balance point, carefully place approximately the middle of the flat side surface of the knife's blade on your extended index finger a couple of inches over a cutting board. Slowly move the knife, so that your finger travels up or down the knife's blade, to find the position on the knife where it is completely balanced by your one finger. At that point place your thumb of your same hand on the opposite side of the blade and wrap your remaining fingers around the handle.

On a good quality knife, this balance point will be approximately on the first inch of where the blade extends from the handle. This is usually because the knife has a full tang, and the weight of this full tang in the handle offsets the weight of the remaining steel in the knife's extended blade. It may seem awkward at first, to grasp the base of the blade in your hand, but after regular practice, it will become comfortable. Holding the knife in other fashions, such as having the index finger extended on the top of the knife when cutting, will reduce the amount of control one has and increase the chance of injury. If you find these instructions on holding a Chef's knife are unclear, I recommend searching the internet to get a visual of this technique.

Placement of the opposite hand (the one holding the food) is also just as vital to prevent injury. One should grasp the product in a claw type fashion, with the finger tips bent inwards and the thumb tucked behind them. Having the finger tips bent in towards the palm of the hand will get them out of harm's way of the knife blade, and thus reduce the risk of injury.

Always practice precision and speed will come in time. Having precise cuts is better than risking an injury. Welcome the chance to practice your knife skills with every opportunity and efficiency will come naturally.

Dear Chef Dez:

Any tips on cutting a loaf of bread horizontally without it being uneven? For example, cutting a full loaf of French bread in half to make garlic bread. Every time I do it, it is never even.

Pam C.
Airdrie, AB

Dear Pam:

After starting the cut, it is important to watch where the top edge of your serrated knife is as it moves along the loaf. Don't watch the part of the knife closest to the handle as it will follow the same even path simultaneously as the top edge. It is closer to where your hand is controlling the knife, and thus less chance for error as long as the knife is even by watching the top edge.

Also be careful to keep your other hand completely flat on the top of the loaf as you cut. Any fingers that could be carelessly hanging down off the side of the loaf are susceptible to being cut accidentally. As an extra precaution, continue to move this hand down the loaf as you cut, keeping it an inch or two away from where the knife is doing the cutting at all times. When you get close to the end of cutting the loaf, move this hand over to the other side of the bread (that has been cut already), to prevent injury as the knife exits the loaf.

French Onion Soup

Originally prepared for Lepp Farm Market <u>www.leppfarmmarket.com</u>
Full colour photo available at www.chefdez.com

"Using a combination of beef broth and red wine, along with the caramelized onions makes this soup very complex in taste. Look for Onion Goggles at your local kitchen supply store to help keep your onion tears at bay."

3 tbsp butter
5 medium onions, halved and sliced thin
3 tbsp brown sugar
1/2 tsp salt
1 baguette
1 cup full bodied red wine
6 & 1/2 cups beef broth
2 bay leaves
2 large sprigs fresh thyme
300g gruyere cheese, grated
Salt & pepper

1. Over medium-high heat, melt the butter in a large pot until foaming.
2. Add the onions, brown sugar, salt and turn the heat to medium. Cook, stirring occasionally, for 30 to 45 minutes until the onions have reduced and caramelized, and they start to brown the bottom of the pot.
3. While the onions are cooking, preheat the oven to 450 degrees Fahrenheit. Slice 12 half-inch, 45 degree slices of the baguette (enough for 2 slices per serving) and place them on a baking sheet. Toast in the oven for 5 minutes and set aside.
4. Once the onions have caramelized, add the wine, broth, bay leaves, and thyme to the pot. Bring to a boil over high heat and then reduce the heat to simmer, uncovered, for 30 minutes to concentrate the flavours. Season to taste with salt & pepper.
5. Remove and discard the bay leaves and thyme sprigs. Ladle the soup into 6 oven-proof bowls. Top each bowl with 2 toasted baguette slices and an equal amount of grate cheese. Broil in the oven until the cheese is melted and golden. Serve immediately.

Makes 6 portions

Green Bean Salad

Recipe created by Katherine Desormeaux (Mrs. Chef Dez)

"A very simple salad for when fresh green beans are at the peak of the season"

6 cups cut green beans, cut diagonally in half, approx 2 inch pieces
1 red bell pepper, cut in similar size/shape as the beans
1/2 cup cut red onion, cut in similar size/shape as the beans
Juice of 1 lemon
1/3 cup extra virgin olive oil
2 tbsp sugar
1 tsp salt

1. Steam the green beans until cooked but still firm, approximately 2 minutes. Immediately plunge them in an ice-water bath to halt the cooking process. Once cold, drain thoroughly.
2. In a large bowl toss the green beans, red pepper and onion together.
3. In a small separate bowl, whisk together the lemon juice, oil, sugar, and salt. Pour over the green bean mixture and toss. Serve immediately.

Makes approximately 7 cups

Rosemary Garlic Quinoa

"Quinoa (pronounced 'keen-wah') is a great grain that is lower in carbohydrates and higher in protein."

2 tbsp canola oil
6 garlic cloves, chopped
2 tbsp chopped fresh rosemary
2 cups quinoa
4 cups water
1 tsp salt
1/2 tsp pepper

1. Add the 2 tbsp canola oil, chopped garlic and rosemary to a pot and cook briefly over medium heat—make sure to not burn the garlic otherwise it will taste bitter. Stir in the quinoa and cook for another 30 seconds. Add the water, salt & pepper and continue to cook on medium to medium-high heat uncovered, stirring occasionally, until all of the liquid has been absorbed/evaporated, approximately 15 to 20 minutes. Re-season to taste if necessary.

Makes approximately 6 side dish portions

South-Western Creamed Corn

Originally prepared for Lepp Farm Market www.leppfarmmarket.com
Full colour photo available at www.chefdez.com

"Make sure you add the lime juice at the very end when the pan is off the heat. This keeps it tasting very fresh and lively."

3 strips of bacon, sliced into ¼ inch pieces
3 tbsp minced onion
1 canned chipotle pepper, minced
2 garlic cloves, minced
5 cups fresh corn kernels or 5 cups frozen (thawed & drained)
1 medium red bell pepper, diced small (approximately 1 cup)
1 & 1/2 tsp salt
1/4 tsp pepper
1 cup whipping cream
1 cup grated old cheddar
Juice of a half lime

1. In a large pan over medium heat, cook the bacon pieces until cooked, but not crisp, approximately 5 minutes.
2. Add the onion, chipotle, and garlic. Stir and cook for 1 minute.
3. Add the corn, bell pepper, salt and pepper. Stir and cook for 2 to 3 minutes.
4. Stir in the cream and cheddar and continue cooking while stirring until slightly thickened to desired consistency, approximately 2 to 3 more minutes.
5. Remove from the heat, stir in the fresh lime juice and serve immediately.

Makes approximately 7 cups

17

What is Classified as a Comfort Food?

We have all heard of the term "comfort food" . . . we in fact have all craved it, smelled the aromas from it in anticipation, and of course eaten it. What is "comfort food" though, exactly? Is it only big bowls of stew-ish type foods on a cold winter day that one eats while wearing pants with a stretchy waistband? Does it exist in climates where it is warm year round? Comfort food can be, and is, whatever you want it to be by what it means to you. That's the beauty of it; if by eating it, it gives you a level of comfort, be it physical or emotional, then it can be considered comfort food.

The physical contentment from eating comfort foods would be the warmth felt by the temperature of the dish, or the spiciness of it, and/or even the mouth feel of the richness about it. However pairing these physical sensations with the psychological satisfaction from eating something considered to be a comfort food, is where I think the true definition lies within people and where the pleasure really comes from.

Comfort food can be a dish that stirs up sentimental feelings for example. Maybe a certain aroma and corresponding flavour is linked to a memory of a place once visited, a special time or celebration in one's life, or of a beloved person. For example, when I smell turkey and stuffing cooking my mind always takes me back in times to when I was a boy and would come in the house from playing outside on a crisp autumn Thanksgiving day. The warm aromas of sage and turkey blanketing every nook and cranny of our old house revealed to me my Mom's selfless efforts made by her that morning. Smell is a huge part of the enjoyment of eating and tasting and it has been scientifically proven that our sense of smell is directly linked to memory. This is also the reason we are turned off by some foods or dishes, because the aromas and related tastes are linked to times of unhappiness or ill feelings.

Recipes of a nostalgic nature may also contribute to be classified as comfort foods. Foods from a certain time period or specific culture that trigger emotions may be enough to sanction it into this classification. For instance, on the 17th of March when our table is filled with classic Irish dishes, it not only feels more fitting, but also fulfilling . . . or comforting. This is just one example of many celebrations that could include, but not limited to, Asian delights on Chinese New Year, incredible Indian food on Dwali, or haggis on Robbie Burns Day . . . yes, there are people that consider even haggis to be comfort food. For those of you not in the Scottish culinary loop, haggis can be defined as a savoury pudding containing a sheep's organs (heart, liver, and lungs for example) and combined with onion, oatmeal, and spices traditionally encased in the sheep's stomach and simmered for hours. I am actually quite fond of it myself on occasion as long as it is served warm; once it gets cold I find the texture loses its appeal.

The feel good sensation of comfort food can also be obtained by simply just loving the taste of something, maybe by that of your favorite type of food or favorite recipe; which literally could translate into almost anything for any one individual. Basically foods that make you feel good because you are consuming something you love to eat. The act of doing so would bring on positive emotions and help to suppress negative feelings, and that alone could be enough to be considered comfort food. Now if this was a column on dietary pros and cons and examining how food addictions can alter lifestyles in a negative way, we would then discuss moderation, balanced diets, and portion control. However, for the sake of the love of the culinary arts we will end it here on a positive note instead.

So, in conclusion, comfort food can be, and is, anything you want it to be, as long as it makes you happy for one reason or another . . . even if it is just temporary.

Dear Chef Dez:

I have heard that "braising" is the best way to make tough meats tender. Do you agree and what is braising?

Alfred S.
Winnipeg, MB

Dear Alfred,

Marinating is a good way too, but I guess if I had to choose I would pick braising. Braising is a combination of dry and moist heat cooking processes. First the meat is seared at a high temperature to create a flavourful crust on the meat and then cooked through in a moist heat environment at a low temperature for a long period of time. The low moist heat is what breaks down and transforms tough connective tissue into mouth-watering tender meals. Seared in a hot pan and then cooked in a covered casserole dish with liquid in a 250 to 300 degree Fahrenheit oven for a few hours would be considered braising. Please keep in mind that this is an example only and would depend on the type and size of meat you are cooking.

Artichoke & Asiago Dip

1 cup mayonnaise
1/2 cup drained minced canned artichokes
50g grated Asiago cheese, approx. 1/2 cup
1/2 to 1 garlic clove, crushed to a paste
1 tsp lemon juice
1/2 tsp salt
1/2 tsp liquid honey
1/2 tsp sweet smoked paprika, optional

1.   Mix everything together and serve with crackers or tortilla chips.

Makes approximately 2 cups

Bacon & Blueberry Salad

"The greens will get a bit wilted from the warm dressing, so only dress them immediately before serving"

Rendered fat from 1/2 pound bacon, approximately 1/2 cup
Reserved cooked bacon, crumbled and set aside
3 tbsp apple cider vinegar
1 to 2 tbsp maple syrup
2 tsp Dijon or grainy mustard
1/2 tsp dried thyme leaves
Fresh cracked pepper, to season
Washed mixed greens or spinach leaves
2 cups fresh blueberries
Sliced or slivered almonds

1. Add the vinegar, syrup, mustard, thyme, and pepper to the rendered bacon fat (make sure that the bacon fat is not too hot or the hot fat will splatter you when you add these ingredients).
2. Heat over medium heat until very warm while stirring together.
3. Serve immediately over your choice of greens and top with blueberries, crumbled reserved bacon, and the almonds.

Makes 4 to 6 portions

Candied Pecans

"Doing these nuts in a pan instead of the oven helps you keep an eye on them before they burn! Great as a topping for salads, cakes, desserts, or just eat them on they're own."

1/4 cup butter
1/3 cup brown sugar
Pinch of salt
2 cups pecan halves

1. Prepare a baking sheet with parchment paper and set aside.
2. Melt the butter in a pan over medium heat to medium/low heat.
3. Add the sugar, salt and pecans and cook, stirring frequently, until the pecans have cooked to the point of turning dark brown (not black), approximately 10 to 15 minutes. Immediately transfer the cooked pecans to the reserved prepared baking sheet to prevent further cooking. Cool in the refrigerator until cold and then separate the nuts with your hands.

Makes 2 cups

Dixie's Baked Beans

"Big thank you to Aunty Dixie for letting us use her incredible baked beans recipe. These are probably the best baked beans you have ever had!"

450g bag dry small white beans, approximately 2 cups
8 cups water

1/2 pound (227g) bacon, chopped
3-284ml cans condensed tomato soup
2 cups water (not needed for slow-cooker method)

355ml can beer
1/2 cup ketchup
1 large onion, diced small
4 to 6 cloves garlic, minced
3/4 cup dark brown sugar
2 celery stalks, finely chopped
2 tsp dry mustard
3 tbsp molasses
1 tsp salt
Pepper to taste

OVEN METHOD
1. Pour the 8 cups water over the beans and let soak overnight—OR—put beans in a pot, add the water, bring to a full boil for 2 minutes, turn off the heat, cover and let sit for 2 hours.
2. Drain the beans and put them in a large oven proof pot. Add all the remaining ingredients and bring to a boil on the stove top. Cover and transfer to a preheated 350 degree Fahrenheit oven. Bake for 4 to 5 hours until beans are tender. Add more liquid if necessary during the cooking process if beans seem dry. Re-season with salt & pepper if necessary before serving.

SLOW-COOKER METHOD
1. Pour the 8 cups water over the beans and let soak overnight—OR—put beans in a pot, add the water, bring to a full boil for 2 minues, turn off the heat, cover and let sit for 2 hours.
2. Drain the beans and put them in large pot. Add all the remaining ingredients (except for the 2 cups of water) and bring to a boil. Transfer to a slow-cooker/crockpot and cook on high for 6 hours, or on low for 8 to 10 hours. Re-season with salt & pepper if necessary before serving.

Guinness Brownies

"These are dark, rich, beautiful brownies with just a slight aftertaste of sweet bitterness from the Guinness. You will love these even if you don't like drinking Guinness."

Butter for the pan
1-440ml can Guinness, room temperature
4 large eggs
1 cup berry (superfine) sugar
3 cups pure semi-sweet chocolate chips (500g bag)
1/2 cup butter
1 cup flour
1 cup cocoa
Ice cream, whipped cream, or icing sugar for serving, optional

1. Preheat oven to 350 degrees. Butter a 9x13 pan.
2. Slowly pour the Guinness into a measuring cup or bowl to let the foam subside.
3. Beat the eggs and sugar together until light and fluffy.
4. In a double boiler, melt the chocolate chips with the butter, stirring until smooth. Remove from heat and add gradually while beating into the egg mixture.
5. Sift the flour and cocoa together.
6. To the chocolate/egg mixture, add the flour/cocoa mixture in three parts alternating with the Guinness in two parts, until well combined. The batter will seem very liquid.
7. Pour into the prepared pan and bake for approximately 30 minutes, or until an inserted toothpick in the centre comes out clean. Remove from the oven and let cool on a wire rack.
8. Cut into a maximum of 24 squares. Serve with ice cream, whip cream, or dust with icing sugar.

Honey Garlic Meatballs

Originally prepared for Lepp Farm Market www.leppfarmmarket.com
Full colour photo available at www.chefdez.com

"Combining two different types of meat gives the meatballs more complex flavour and seasoned with Chinese 5 Spice powder they are perfect with this sauce. Enjoy!"

1 pound (454g) ground chuck
1 pound (454g) lean ground pork
2 large eggs
1/2 cup fine bread crumbs
1/4 cup minced onion
2 tbsp finely crushed or minced garlic
1 tbsp Chinese 5 Spice powder
2 tsp salt
1 tsp pepper

Sauce
1 cup + 2 tbsp beef broth
3/4 cup dark brown sugar
1/2 cup liquid honey
6 tbsp soy sauce
3 tbsp cornstarch
1.5 tbsp finely crushed garlic
1/2 tsp salt

1. Preheat oven to 400 degrees Fahrenheit. Spray a baking sheet with baking spray and set aside.
2. In a large bowl, combine the chuck, pork, eggs, bread crumbs, onion, garlic, 5 spice, 2 tsp salt & the pepper. Mix until thoroughly combined into a homogenous mixture. Roll bits of the mixture into small meatballs approximately 3/4 inch in size and place them on the prepared baking sheet. You should have approximately 45 to 50

meatballs. Bake in the preheated oven for approximately 20 minutes, or until their internal temperature reaches 160 degrees Fahrenheit (71 degrees Celsius).

3. While the meatballs are cooking, prepare the sauce by placing the beef broth, brown sugar, honey, soy sauce, cornstarch, garlic and half tsp salt in a medium heavy-bottomed pot. Place on medium-high heat and bring to a boil stirring occasionally. When it just starts to boil stir constantly until it has reached a full rolling boil. It must reach a full boil to activate the cornstarch thickener fully. Remove from the heat and set aside.

4. Place the cooked meatballs on paper towel temporarily to remove some of the fat. Transfer the meatballs to a serving dish, cover with the sauce and serve immediately with or without cooked rice.

Makes 45 to 50, 3/4 inch meatballs

Braised Lamb Shanks in Barbeque Sauce

Full colour photo available at www.chefdez.com

"In the oven or a pressure cooker, either way these lamb shanks are incredibly tender and flavourful"

3 small lamb shanks (1kg total)
2-3 tbsp canola oil
Salt & pepper
3 sprigs fresh rosemary, chopped
6 garlic cloves, chopped
3 shallots, chopped—or—1/3 cup small diced onion
2 tbsp minced fresh ginger
1 cup red wine
3 to 6 tbsp of your favourite Barbeque Sauce
1/2 tsp salt
1/2 tsp pepper
1 to 1 & 1/2 tsp white sugar
1 tbsp cornstarch dissolved in 2 tbsp red wine

OVEN METHOD

1. Preheat oven to 300 degrees Fahrenheit.
2. Heat an oven proof pan over medium-high heat. Coat the lamb shanks with 1 tbsp of the oil and season with salt and pepper. When the pan is hot, add 1 tbsp of oil to the pan and then sear the lamb shanks on all sides and ends.
3. Once the lamb is seared, remove the lamb from the pan and remove pan from the heat to cool down a bit. Score the shanks deeply in a number of spots and stuff with rosemary.
4. Add one more tbsp of oil to the pan (if needed) along with the garlic, shallots, and ginger. Cook for 1 minute. If the pan is too cool, place it on medium heat.
5. Add the wine to the pan and stir to deglaze.
6. Add the lamb shanks back to the pan and spread 1 to 2 tbsp of barbeque sauce on the top of each shank.
7. Cover the pan and bake in the oven for approximately 90 minutes until the meat is tender and mostly releasing from the bones.
8. Remove the lamb shanks from the pan and set aside to rest.
9. While lamb is resting, finish the sauce by adding salt, pepper, and dissolved cornstarch. Bring to a boil on the stovetop to thicken and then serve over the lamb shanks.

PRESSURE COOKER METHOD

1. Preheat pressure cooker pot over medium-high heat. Coat the lamb shanks with 1 tbsp of the oil and season with salt and pepper. When the pot is hot, add 1 tbsp of oil to the pot and then sear the lamb shanks on all sides and ends.
2. Once the lamb is seared, remove the lamb from the pot and remove pot from the heat to cool down a bit. Score the shanks deeply in a number of spots and stuff with rosemary.
3. Add one more tbsp of oil to the pot (if needed) along with the garlic, shallots, and ginger. Cook for 1 minute. If the pot is too cool, place it on medium heat.
4. Add the wine to the pot and stir to deglaze.
5. Add the lamb shanks back to the pot and spread 1 to 2 tbsp of barbeque sauce on the top of each shank.

6. Close the pressure cooker, turn the heat to high, and cook under pressure for 30 minutes, reducing heat and timing from when pressure is reached. Remove from the heat source, and allow pressure to drop naturally. Open the pressure cooker once pressure has dropped completely. Remove the lamb shanks from the pressure cooker and set aside to rest.

7. While lamb is resting, finish the sauce by adding salt, pepper, and dissolved cornstarch. Bring to a boil to thicken and then serve over the lamb shanks.

Makes approximately 3-4 portions

Maple Mashed Sweet Potatoes

Originally prepared for Lepp Farm Market www.leppfarmmarket.com
Full colour photo available at www.chefdez.com

1.5kg Sweet Potatoes (orange fleshed yams), peeled & cubed 1/2 inch
1/2 cup butter
2.5 tsp salt
1/4 tsp pepper
1/3 cup maple syrup
Chopped pecans or candied pecans for garnish, optional

1. Steam the sweet potato cubes for approximately 20 to 25 minutes until soft.
2. Mash the sweet potatoes with the butter, salt and pepper until smooth.
3. Mix in the maple syrup thoroughly, and serve immediately. Garnish with optional pecan pieces.

Makes approximately 6 cups

Pear & Cranberry Cobbler

Recipe created by Katherine Desormeaux (Mrs. Chef Dez)
Full colour photo available at www.chefdez.com

Butter for the pie plate
6 cups peeled and 1/2 inch diced pears
1 cup fresh (or thawed from frozen) cranberries
1/3 cup packed brown sugar
1 tbsp cornstarch
1 tbsp lemon or lime juice
1/4 tsp ground nutmeg
1 cup all-purpose flour
1/2 cup whole wheat flour
2 tbsp sugar
2 tsp baking powder
1 tsp baking soda
1/2 tsp salt
1/4 cup frozen butter
3/4 cup buttermilk
1/4 tsp chopped lemon zest or lemon extract

1. Preheat oven to 400 degrees Fahrenheit and prepare a 9 inch pie plate by buttering it.
2. Mix the pears, cranberries, brown sugar, cornstarch, lemon or lime juice, and the nutmeg together and spread into the prepared pie plate.
3. In a separate bowl, mix the all-purpose flour, whole wheat flour, sugar, baking powder, baking soda, and salt together. Grate in the frozen butter with a cheese grater and toss in. Add the buttermilk and the lemon and mix until just combined. Drop by spoonfuls onto the fruit.
4. Bake for approximately 35 minutes until topping and fruit are cooked. Serve warm with ice cream or whipped cream.

Makes one 9-inch cobbler

Rubbed & Sauced Baby Back Ribs

Originally prepared for Lepp Farm Market www.leppfarmmarket.com
Full colour photo available at www.chefdez.com

"The flavours of both the rub and the sauce come together perfectly to create Ribs to die for!"

1/4 brown sugar (not golden sugar)
3 tbsp sweet smoked paprika
1 tbsp chilli powder
1 tbsp garlic powder
1 tbsp onion powder
1 tsp celery salt
1 tsp salt
1 tsp pepper
1/2 tsp ground cumin
4 racks of Pork Baby Back Ribs
1 & 1/2 cups ketchup
1/2 cup Jack Daniels whiskey
3/4 cup brown sugar (not golden sugar)
4 garlic cloves, minced very fine
1/4 cup apple cider vinegar
1 tbsp Worcestershire sauce
1 tsp liquid smoke
1 tsp salt

1. In a small bowl, mix the 1/4 cup brown sugar, paprika, chilli powder, garlic powder, onion powder, celery salt, 1 tsp salt, pepper, and the cumin.
2. Preheat your BBQ on high heat.
3. Preheat your oven to 300 degrees F.
4. Rub the spice mix (from step 1) liberally onto the racks of ribs. Sear them on the BBQ just until both sides of the ribs are mostly caramelized. Remove the ribs and place them side-by-side on a baking sheet large enough to accommodate all 4 racks.

5. Pour ¾ (three quarters) cup water directly onto this baking sheet (don't pour on the ribs), and then cover and tightly seal this baking sheet completely with aluminum foil. It is important to make sure that no steam can escape from the pan—this will ensure a perfect braising environment to create tender meat.

6. Bake at 300 degrees F for 1 & 1/2 hours.

7. Lower the oven temperature to 250 degrees F and bake for another 1 & 1/2 hours.

8. While the ribs are cooking, make the sauce. In a medium pot, combine the ketchup, Jack Daniels, 3/4 cup brown sugar, garlic, vinegar, Worcestershire, liquid smoke, and the 1 tsp salt. Heat over medium-high heat until boiling, stirring constantly. Lower the heat to low and simmer, uncovered, for 30 minutes, stirring occasionally. Set aside, off the heat, when done.

9. ALL OF THE FOLLOWING STEPS MUST BE DONE CAREFULLY, AS THE RIBS ARE NOW SO TENDER THAT THEY WILL FALL OFF THE BONES.

10. Pierce/tear a corner of the aluminum foil and carefully pour out (and discard) the water.

11. Turn your oven to broil.

12. Remove and discard the aluminum foil. Spoon the sauce liberally on the tops of the rib racks and gently spread to make sure they are well coated.

13. Broil on the top rack of the oven until the sauce starts to caramelize.

14. Gently remove the ribs off the tray and transfer onto plates (or a serving platter) by sliding a long utensil (tongs, for example) underneath each rack in order to not disturb the shape of the racks.

Makes approximately 4 to 8 portions

Sour Cream Mashed Potatoes

3 pounds russet potatoes, peeled
1 tsp salt
1/2 tsp freshly ground black pepper
1/4 to 1/3 cup butter
1/2 cup sour cream
Fresh chopped parsley, optional

1. Cut the potatoes into 1/2-inch cubes and steam them over boiling water for 20 to 25 minutes until tender.
2. Discard the water and transfer the steamed potatoes to the hot pot. Add the salt, pepper and butter and mash by hand. Stir in the sour cream, and season to taste with more salt & pepper if desired. Serve immediately. Finish with fresh chopped parsley if desired.

Al denté—Italian for *"to the tooth"*. The term most commonly used to describe the cooking of pasta, meaning it should not be overcooked and have a bit of resistance when bitten into.

Beef Stock Paste—beef stock/broth that has been concentrated down to a paste consistency. Allows one to add intense flavour without adding liquid to a recipe.

Chicken Stock Paste—chicken stock/broth that has been concentrated down to a paste consistency. Allows one to add intense flavour without adding liquid to a recipe.

Chipotle Peppers—are smoked jalapeno peppers and are usually packaged in cans.

Deglaze—to remove the browned bits (fond) in a hot pan by adding a liquid. This lifts the fond off of the pan and it becomes part of the sauce/finished dish.

Double Boiler—a pot or saucepan that has an insert that sits above the water level. This allows to cook with steam as a heat source.

Dredge—to drag through dry ingredients to coat.

Emulsifier—an ingredient, such as egg yolks or anything made from mustard seed, that helps bind oil and liquids together.

Frenched Rack of Lamb—bones on the rack have been cleaned of tissue/fat for better presentation.

Juniper Berries—are usually sold dried and used to flavor meats, sauces, stuffings, etc. They are too bitter to eat raw and they are generally crushed to release their flavor. These pungent berries are what give gin its distinct flavor.

Ketjap Manis—is basically sweet soy sauce. Look for it at your local Asian grocery or down the Asian foods aisle in your major supermarket. If you can't find it you can substitute it with 4 tablespoons of soy sauce mixed with 3 tablespoons of sugar.

Quinoa—is superior to other grains because it is a complete protein, containing 8 essential amino acids. It is actually a seed, not a grain, and is gluten free. It is highly appreciated for its nutritional value, as its protein content is very high. Unlike wheat or rice (which are low in lysine), quinoa contains a balanced set of essential amino acids for humans, making it an unusually complete foodstuff. Quinoa is higher than wheat, corn or white rice in iron, phosphorus, and calcium. It is also a good source of dietary fiber and phosphorus and is high in magnesium.
When cooked, the grain itself is soft and delicate, but the germ is crunchy, creating a delicious combination of flavour and texture.
It is an excellent meat substitute in vegetarian dishes. It can be used in stir-fries, soups, stews, salads and many more of your favourite recipes.
Quinoa is an easy food to prepare, has a pleasantly light, fluffy texture when cooked, and its mild, slightly nutty flavor makes it an excellent alternative to white rice or couscous.

Reduce/Reduction—to decrease in volume by the process of evaporation. As steam rises from a pan/pot, water is being released and the residual product has intensified flavour and is smaller in quantity.

Sambal Oelek—a crushed chili product that comes in a liquid/paste form. It can usually be found in any major grocery store down the Asian food isle or Imported foods isle.

Shallot—a variety of onion that is smaller and milder than regular onions.

Tahini—Sesame Seed Paste

tbsp—abbreviation for tablespoon.

tsp—abbreviation for teaspoon.

Tzatziki—a Greek dipping sauce made from yogurt, cucumber, fresh dill and garlic. Traditionally served on Greek souvlaki.

Vegetable Stock Paste—vegetable stock/broth that has been concentrated down to a paste consistency. Allows one to add intense flavour without adding liquid to a recipe.

Zest—the coloured outer peel of citrus fruit, not the white bitter pith on the underside of the peel. A tool called a zester or a fine-toothed food grater will help remove this efficiently.

A

Appetizers

B

Beef

C

Chicken

Desserts

Dressings

Lamb

Muffins

Pasta

Pork

Potatoes

Salads

Salsas

Sauces

Sausages

Seafood

T

V

Conversion Chart

Volume measurements

3 teaspoons	=	1 tablespoon
2 tablespoons	=	1 fluid ounce
2 fluid ounces	=	¼ (one quarter) cup
¼ (one quarter) cup	=	4 tablespoons
8 fluid ounces	=	1 cup or 16 tablespoons
1 litre	=	4 cups or 32 fluid ounces

Weight Measurements

227 grams	=	½ (one half) pound
454 grams	=	1 pound
1 pound	=	16 ounces (not fluid ounces)
1 kilogram	=	2.2 pounds

Oven Temperature Measurements (Fahrenheit to Celsius)

225 degrees F	=	105 degrees C
250 degrees F	=	120 degrees C
275 degrees F	=	135 degrees C
300 degrees F	=	150 degrees C
325 degrees F	=	165 degrees C
350 degrees F	=	175 degrees C
375 degrees F	=	190 degrees C
400 degrees F	=	205 degrees C
425 degrees F	=	220 degrees C
450 degrees F	=	230 degrees C
475 degrees F	=	245 degrees C